11+

Non-Verbal Reasoning Success

Targeted Practice

Neil R Williams

Purpose of the book

This book provides structured practice in the final weeks leading up to the 11+ tests, focusing on the most important non-verbal reasoning skills.

Because your time is valuable this book will…

1 help you to identify the skills where you are weakest

2 help plan your time to target these skills and recap skills where you are more confident

3 provide a clear explanation of what you need to be able to do

4 lead you through typical questions

5 give you opportunities to practise your skills

6 provide test practice at the end of each stage

7 direct you back to the skills where you are less confident for your final practice.

The book is designed to help you complete your practice in **four weeks**, once you have assessed your current skills.

You are provided with the following tools to help you plan how much time to spend on each skill:

- **The Placement test**, covering the most important 11+ skills. The questions are designed to be challenging and are of a similar standard to the more difficult questions in the 11+ tests. *The Placement test* is timed so that you can check you are working at the speed expected for the 11+ tests.

- **The Placement test answer grid** directs you to the relevant skills pages in the book, covering all the areas you have been tested on.

- **A Practice planner** (built into the *Placement test answer grid*) enables you to plan your time efficiently, based on the feedback from your *Placement test*. It allows more time for skills you have highlighted for further practice and a short amount of time for skills that simply need refreshing.

- **The skills practice** pages are designed to build confidence in the key non-verbal reasoning skills needed in the 11+ tests. Each page covers a set of skills with step-by-step instructions on how to tackle related questions with Skills practice boxes to test your understanding.

- **Practice tests** at the end of each chapter cover the skills you have just worked through. The questions are challenging and represent difficult problems you may face in the 11+ tests. The tests are timed so that you can check you are working at the speed expected; in the 11+ tests you will have, on average, 30 seconds per question plus reading time.

- **Practice tests answer grids** are provided for you to record your scores from the *Practice tests* and to help you decide which skills you may need to look at again in your final preparation for the 11+ tests.

- **A Countdown grid** is provided for you to record the skills you want to practise again before the 11+ tests, so that you can plan your time effectively.

Timing the Practice tests

You should time the *Practice tests* yourself (aiming for the 'Target time' at the top of each test) to make sure you are working at the speed expected for the 11+ tests. If you feel that you need more time, complete the tests and make a note of the time you have taken.

Plan to retake any tests that you didn't complete in the suggested time as part of your final practice. Because these tests are challenging, you are allocated on average, one minute per question but are likely to have only 30 seconds in the 11+ tests.

Countdown *grid*

Follow the instructions on page 5 to fill in and use this grid.

Skill	Page	Review ✗	Time (mins)	Completed ✓
Question types and strategies	6			
Making connections				
Common connections	10		7	✓
Connections of direction, angle and symmetry	11		15	✓
Finding similarities and differences	13	✗	7	✓
Spotting distractions	14		7	✓
Making connections *test*	15	Retake	15	✓

Contents

Taking the *Placement test*...

Take the *Placement test* in this book to help you identify the skills you need to concentrate on and plan your practice time effectively. Follow the instructions below to take the test.

1 Begin by taking the Placement test

- Find a quiet place to work.
- Assemble the materials you will need before beginning: a pen, pencil, eraser, pencil sharpener, ruler, timer and spare paper. If the school you are applying to allows you to use tracing paper and a mirror in your 11+ test, use these for your Placement test as well.
- Turn to the *Placement test* on pages 45–50.
- Allow **45** minutes to take the test.

2 Mark the Placement test

- Go to the *Placement test answers* on page 54 and score your completed paper by filling in the blank boxes in the 'Mark' column on your test paper:
  - There is one mark per question.
  - **There are no half marks.**
- Now turn to the *Placement test answer grid* on page 51 and fill in the blue *Test results* section:
  - Put a cross in the 'Error' column for each question you answered **incorrectly**.

13		
14	✕	Number and proportion
15		
16	✕	Moving and connecting sha
17		
18		Reflections in vertical lines
19		Reflections in horizontal an

- Count up the boxes **without** crosses in, and put this number in the blue 'Total' box. This is your total test score.

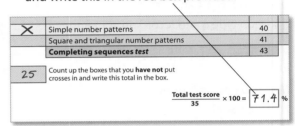

- Calculate your percentage score as directed and write this in the red box provided.

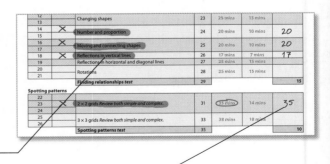

Although the *Placement test* is designed to test your ability to answer the more difficult questions in the 11+ tests, it is also a useful indicator of your progress. A score of 70% or above should give you confidence for the 11+ tests.

Now you have the results, you can begin to plan your time.

1 Fill in the Practice planner

The *Practice planner* forms the right-hand section of the *Placement test answer grid* on page 51. The time needed to completely review each skill is listed in the 'To do' column; the time needed to recap skills already mastered is listed in the 'Achieved' column.

The following instructions explain how to work out the time you should allow to practise these skills:

- Use a highlighter to mark every skill that you have put a cross against.
- Transfer the time needed to complete these skills from the 'To do' column to the 'Time' column.

- Work down the 'Achieved' column to transfer the time needed to complete the remaining skills (the skills where you have answered the questions correctly) to the 'Time' column:

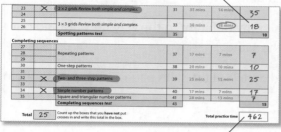

- Add up the time for each section, including the *Question types* and *strategies* at the top and all the *Practice tests*. (The suggested times for these tests are already recorded in the 'Time' column.)

2 Planning your time

You now know the total number of minutes you will need to work through the skills in this book.

- Divide the number of minutes by 60 to find the number of hours.
- Work out how many hours you need to spend each week:
  - Split your time between the number of weeks you have available.
  - Aim to complete your practice at least one week before the 11+ tests to give you time to go over any skills you feel you would like to look at again.
- Monitor your time to make sure that you are working to the suggested timings and adjust the amount of time you allow if necessary.

3 Practising the skills

Work through your practice using your *Practice planner* in the following way:

- Complete a chapter before moving on by...
  - working through the highlighted skills thoroughly and answering the *Skills practice* questions. (The answers are on pages 54–55.)
  - quickly reading through the remaining skills, and answering these *Skills practice* questions as well (if you are short of time, try the *Skills practice* questions and only read the skills text if you can't work out the correct answer).
- Complete the *Practice test* at the end of the chapter to double-check that you are confident in the skills.
- Mark your answers to the *Practice tests* using the answers on pages 55–56.

- Complete the *Practice tests answer grids* on pages 52–53 to help you plan your remaining practice time:
  - Make notes about any of the questions you found challenging in the 'Notes' column.
  - Complete the 'Review' and 'Achieved' columns to indicate whether you want to look at the skills again.
  - Add up your score and work out your percentage.
- A score of 70% or above in these challenging tests should give you confidence for the 11+ tests.

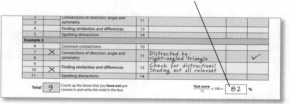

4 Completing your practice

After you have completed all your planned practice, you will probably have a few skills that you want to go back to. You should have recorded these skills on the *Practice tests answer grids* in the 'Review' column. The *Countdown grid* inside the back cover of this book is provided to help you to plan this final review:

- From reviewing your *Practice tests answer grids*, put a cross in the *Countdown grid* 'Review' column to indicate the skills you are going to look at again.

  Highlight 'Retake' in the 'Review' column for any *Practice tests* you would like to take again.
- Fill in the 'Time' column for these skills and tests with the amount of time printed in grey; the *Practice test* timings are a guide to the speed you should now be achieving.
- Add up your total time to plan your final practice.
- Complete your final practice programme and tick the 'Completed' column for each skill as you finish it.
- Plan a break before your 11+ tests so that you are feeling awake and ready to face the challenge.

Feel confident that you are well prepared, and stay positive. **This is your chance to shine!**

Taking the 11+ test

You may find in the 11+ tests that the questions are read out to you and that you are then given an allocated amount of time to complete the questions before moving on to the next section.

Non-verbal reasoning tests are usually broken up into five or six sections. Each section will have questions of just one type in it. This makes the test a little easier as you can get into a rhythm for each section much more readily.

Some of the question types in this book may look slightly different to the way they are laid out in the 11+ test, but you will find that the skills are the same.

This section covers the common question types and details of the skills pages that relate to them.

You must be able to...
- identify the type of question you have been given
- use appropriate methods to tackle each type of question
- follow instructions to give your answer correctly and clearly.

1 Odd one out

Example 1

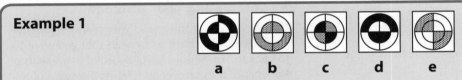

a   b   c   d   e

When you are working with *odd one out* questions, you simply need to look at the images and decide which one of them doesn't quite fit with the rest. Look at Example 1 above.

Each shape is made from eight segments, four on the outside and four on the inside:

- The first shape has alternating black and white segments.
- The second has an even number of spotted and white segments.
- The third has white, spotted and black segments.
- The fourth has an even number of black and white segments.
- The fifth shape has alternating white and spotted segments.

The next step is to find the odd one out:

- Shape **c** seems to stand out as all of the outer segments are white and there are two different types of shading on the inner segments.
- All four of the other shapes have half of their segments in white and half as either spotted or black. Half of the outer segments are white, and half of the inner segments are white.

Shape **c** is the odd one out because the other shapes have two outer segments in white and two inner segments in white but **c** does not.

Skills practice ⟫⟫⟫

This is a skill you can practise with a friend.

From a normal deck of playing cards, pick out four cards that follow a rule. It could be the suit, the colour, odd numbers, even numbers or picture cards. Then pick one card that does not follow the rule. Can your friend spot it? Get your friend to pick a rule and five cards for you.

You can make the game harder by having two rules.

Practice links

*Skills needed for **odd one out** questions:*
Making connections, pages 10–14

2 Most like

Example 2

a   b   c   d   e

Most like questions can be some of the most difficult to answer as you have to decide which connection is the most important.

In these questions you will be shown two or three images on the left that are related by at least one connection. You then have to pick one image to join that group.

In Example 2 above, there are three images that all look like random shapes. However, when you look closely they do have some similarities:

● The first shape has five sides, four acute angles and one reflex angle.

● The second shape has five sides, three acute angles, one obtuse angle and one reflex angle.

● The third shape has five sides, two acute angles, two obtuse angles and one reflex angle.

The **two** connections are that the shapes all have five sides and one reflex angle. It is possible that only one connection is relevant and that the other is a distraction.

Describing the features of each possible answer in the same way helps you to work out which option is correct:

● Shape **a** has three sides and no reflex angles.

● Shape **b** has five sides and no reflex angles.

● Shape **c** has seven sides and two reflex angles.

● Shape **d** has four sides and no reflex angles.

● Shape **e** has four sides and no reflex angles.

None of the options has a single reflex angle so it looks like that is a distraction. The connection you are looking for is a shape with five sides. Only shape **b** has five sides, so that is the correct answer.

Fast facts

An acute angle is less than 90°.

An obtuse angle is between 90° and 180°.

A reflex angle is greater than 180°.

Practice links

*Skills needed for **most like** questions:*

Making connections, pages 10–14

Finding relationships, pages 23–28

3 Grid questions

Example 3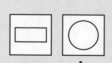

a   b   c   d   e

While a lot of the questions you see use boxes, grid questions take this one step further and put the boxes together to make either 2 × 2 or 3 × 3 grids. Within the grid one box will be empty and you have to pick the box that should fill it from the five options given.

These questions can use a wide range of connections. They commonly use reflections, which are easy to see in the grid as the grid lines give you the mirror line. More complex problems have two or three changes happening between the boxes, often with a number of shapes within each box.

Look at Example 3 above and see if you can work out which of the possible answers is correct. This example is fully worked through on page 31 where the Spotting patterns section begins.

Practice links

*Skills needed for **grid questions**:*

Making connections, pages 10–14

Finding relationships, pages 23–28

Spotting patterns, pages 31–34

④ Repeat the changes

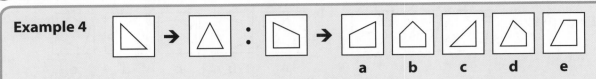

In *repeat the changes* questions the answer can often look quite different from the original question. The reason is that you are shown two images to begin with and are asked to work out what was done to the first image to get to the second. You then have to apply those changes to a third image to come up with a final answer.

The skill in *repeat the changes* questions is to work out the connection between the first two shapes before applying this to the third.

Look at Example 4 above:

● The first shape is a right-angled triangle.

● The second shape is an equilateral triangle.

● Both triangles have the same length base, which is parallel to the bottom of the box.

Fast facts

An equilateral triangle has three sides of equal length and all three angles measuring 60°.

A quadrilateral is any four-sided shape.

Think about the difference between the shapes: the top point of the triangle has moved to the middle of the box.

● Now look at the third box, to see what sort of shape you have been asked to work with: the third shape is an irregular quadrilateral.

● Consider what the shape will look like if the same change is applied to this shape: if the top point moves it will remain an irregular quadrilateral with the same length base parallel to the bottom of the box, but the top point will be moved to the middle of the box.

Shape **d** is the correct answer.

Practice links

*Skills needed for **repeat the changes** questions:*

Making connections, pages 10–14

Finding relationships, pages 23–28

⑤ Breaking codes

Example 5

| DV | DW | CV | BX | ? |

Breaking codes is a unique question type that appears in almost every non-verbal reasoning test. The reason it's unique is that it uses letters for the codes you need to break; no other question type has letter codes within the questions.

You'll be shown five images like Example 5 above:

● Every image will have a code either underneath it or beside it. Those codes will contain one, two or three letters.

● Each letter in the code represents a different feature within the image. As that feature changes so will the letter. The first letter of each image will link to one feature, the second to another and so on.

● All you need to do is break the code and work out what all the letters mean so that you can pick the right code from the five options you are given.

Try to work out the answer code for Example 5 without having the possible answers. This example is fully worked through on page 17 where the Breaking codes section begins.

Practice links

*Skills needed for **breaking codes** questions:*

Making connections, pages 10–14

Breaking codes, pages 17–20

6 Complete the sequence

Example 6

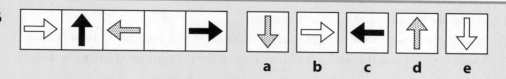

By far the most common question type is *complete the sequence*. In these questions you are usually shown five boxes. Four of them have an image and one of them is empty. The empty box can be anywhere within the sequence. It is easier if it's the first or last box that is empty as you'll have four images in a row to work out the pattern from. The hardest questions have the middle box as the empty one.

The first thing to do is to work out what is changing as you go from one box to the next:

- The arrow is rotating 90° anticlockwise.
- The shading changes from white to black to spotted to *something* to black.

The shading change sounds like a big clue, but you need to ask what that missing something could be:

- The second and fifth boxes have black arrows, so there's a good chance that the shading in the first box should match the shading in the fourth box. This means the arrow in there should be white.

- If the arrow is going anticlockwise it should end up pointing down in the fourth box.
- Putting the clues together, you want a white arrow that is pointing down.

The correct answer is option **e**.

Skills practice ›››

Have a look at the sequence in the example. Continue the pattern until you get an image that looks like the arrow in the first box.

How many arrows do you end up with in the complete sequence?

Practice links

Skills needed for **complete the sequence** *questions:*

Making connections, pages 10–14

Finding relationships, pages 23–28

Completing sequences, pages 37–42

Recording your answers

Generally all of the questions in non-verbal reasoning tests are multiple choice, so you should not have to draw any unusual-looking shapes. However, there are three main ways that you'll be asked to give your answer:

- Circle the answer on the question paper.
- Underline the answer on the question paper.
- Mark the answer on a grid on a separate answer sheet.

If you have ever watched someone fill out a National Lottery play slip, you will know how marking answers on a grid works. You just have to shade/fill in a small box for whichever answer you want to pick. These sheets get fed into a computer, which means they can be checked faster.

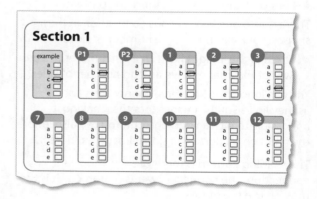

You must be able to...

 recognise the common connection types

 identify the image that doesn't share a connection in a group of regular shapes

 identify the image that doesn't share a connection in a group of irregular shapes.

Example

Look at the five images. Work out what connects four of the images and makes the other image the odd one out. Circle the letter under the image *most unlike* the others.

a   b   c   d   e

① Recognising the common connection types

A connection is something that two or more images have in common such as the number of corners, the shading, the pattern of lines, the shape or size.

Sometimes you will see two common connections and you will need to decide which is the most important connection. Most common connection questions ask you to find one image that doesn't share a connection with the others; the 'odd one out'.

② Identifying the 'odd one out' in a group of regular shapes

Look at the five shapes in the example:

- All of the shapes have straight lines.
- All of the shapes are regular.
- All of the shapes have solid outlines.
- Four of the images have the same pattern.

There is also one less obvious connection in these shapes. Look carefully at the number of sides:

- Three of the images have an even number of sides. Two of the images have an odd number of sides.

You can ignore the first three connections above as they link all of the images together, making it impossible to pick an odd one out. You can also ignore the final connection as no single image is different.

The shading pattern is therefore the important connection. The correct answer is option **c** as it is the most unlike the others.

Fast facts

Regular shapes are shapes where all the lines are the same length and the angles are the same size. Squares and equilateral triangles are both regular shapes.

③ Identifying the 'odd one out' in a group of irregular shapes

a   b   c   d   e

In this set of shapes, there are no shading patterns to consider:

- All of the shapes are made up of straight lines.
- All of the lines are solid.
- None of the shapes are regular.

These connections do not help as they refer to all of the shapes, so you need to look at each shape in more detail. With questions involving irregular shapes it is often a good idea to count the number of sides or types of angles in each shape. This also applies when there is more than one shape in each box; these can be regular or irregular.

Look at the Skills practice to see if you can solve this common connections problem.

⚠ Watch out! 》》》》

Patterns and shading

There are a wide range of shading patterns that can be used in non-verbal reasoning questions; some have lines, some have blocked patterns and some have spots. There can also be subtle variations with vertical, horizontal and diagonal lines counting as different patterns. The lines around the images may also have different patterns such as dots or dashes.

Skills practice 》》》

Count the number of sides and the number of each type of angle in the five irregular shapes above to find which shape is the odd one out.

Connections of direction, angle and symmetry

You must be able to...
- identify connections that involve direction
- identify connections that involve angle
- identify connections that involve symmetry.

Example 1

　　　　　　　　　　　　　　　　　　a　　　b　　　c　　　d　　　e

Look at the two images on the left. Decide what makes these two images similar to each other. Now find the image on the right that is *most like* the two images on the left. Circle the letter under the correct answer.

1 Identifying connections that involve direction

Questions involving direction will often use arrows as they clearly point in a particular way. Along with the direction, the style of the arrow head and the number of fins on the tail can be used as connections.

Looking at the directions

Look closely at the two images on the left in Example 1 above and work out what the connection between their directions might be:

- The first arrow is pointing down and to the right.
- The second arrow is pointing down and to the left.
- Both arrows are pointing downwards.

Checking to see if the direction fits

Only having two images to work with can make it easy to find a general direction, but remember that sometimes you will be given three images to compare. Now check the possible answers to see which ones are pointing downwards:

- Options **a**, **b**, **d** and **e** are pointing upwards.
- Option **c** is pointing downwards.
- The correct answer is option **c**. It is most like the two images on the left.

2 Identifying connections that involve angle

Example 2

　　　　　　　　　　　　　　　　　　a　　　b　　　c　　　d　　　e

Look at the three images on the left. Decide what makes these three images similar to each other. Now find the image on the right that is *most like* the three images on the left. Circle the letter under the correct answer.

When two lines connect you get an angle. Angles can be acute, obtuse, reflex or right angles. Where angle is the connection you will be looking for the same number of angles of a certain type within all of the images.

Identifying the angles

Look at the angles in the three images on the left in Example 2 to see if there is a connection:

- The first image has three acute angles.
- The second image has three acute angles.
- The third image has three acute angles.

All of the images have three acute angles so this is your connection.

Checking the possible answers

Have a look at the five possible answers to see what sorts of angle they have:

- Option **a** has three acute angles.
- Options **b**, **d** and **e** have a right angle.
- Option **c** has an obtuse angle.

There is only one option that could match – option **a** is the correct answer.

③ Identifying connections that involve symmetry

Example 3

a   b   c   d   e

Look at the three images on the left. Decide what makes these three images similar to each other. Now find the image on the right that is *most like* the three images on the left. Circle the letter under the correct answer.

In non-verbal reasoning questions you should think of symmetry as being *within* an image and reflection being a reflection of a *whole* image.

Symmetry *within* images is one of the least common connections. This is because finding shapes with an equal number of lines of symmetry can be difficult. In Example 3 above you will see groups of shapes. These sorts of groups are also seen in questions where the number of corners is the connection, so be careful.

Finding the line of symmetry

There are two lines of symmetry that may be used in these questions: a *vertical* line of symmetry where everything on the left is matched to what is on the right, and a *horizontal* line of symmetry where everything at the top is matched to the bottom. Have a look at the three images and decide which sort of symmetry each one has:

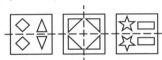

- The first image has a horizontal line of symmetry.
- The second image has a horizontal line of symmetry and a vertical line of symmetry.
- The third image has a horizontal line of symmetry.

All of the images have horizontal lines of symmetry so this is your connection.

Checking the possible answers

Have a look at the five possible answers to see if they have any lines of symmetry:

- Option **a** has no lines of symmetry.
- Option **b** has a vertical line of symmetry.
- Option **c** has a horizontal line of symmetry.
- Option **d** has no lines of symmetry.
- Option **e** has no lines of symmetry.

There is only one option that could match – option **c** is the correct answer.

 Watch out!

Heads and tails

Questions that use arrows can have several different connections, including the head and tail styles. With so many possibilities, make sure you take enough time to find the relevant connection so that you can avoid making simple mistakes.

Quick tips

Watch out for triangles and stars when looking for symmetry within an image . These shapes are easily missed but can give a clue to the direction of symmetry.

Fast facts

Remember that a reflection is not the same as a rotation of 180°.

Skills practice

Find a small mirror, a pencil, some tracing paper and some scrap paper.

Put the tracing paper over the three boxes below and try reflecting each box in a vertical mirror line. You can put the scrap paper between the page and the tracing paper to cover the other boxes.

Use the mirror to check your connection and decide which shape is the odd one out.

a   b   c

Finding similarities and differences

You must be able to...

- identify the similarities and differences between single shapes
- identify the similarities and differences between groups of shapes
- identify the similarities and differences between segmented shapes.

Example

Look at the five images. Work out what connects *four* of the images and makes the other image the odd one out. Circle the letter under the image *most unlike* the others.

a   b   c   d   e

1 Working with single shapes

The simplest comparison you will have to make is between individual shapes. You should consider...

- the shape itself
- the number of sides or corners
- the line and shading styles
- the angles.

Identifying the similarities

Look closely at the five images in the example above and see how many similarities you can find:

- All the images are of triangles.
- All the images are shaded white.

Identifying the differences

Now look at the images again and see how many differences you can find:

- Triangles **a**, **c**, **d** and **e** are equilateral triangles. Triangle **b** is a right-angled triangle.
- Triangles **a** and **d** have solid sides while triangles **b**, **c** and **e** have dashed sides.

The odd one out is **b** as this is the only triangle with a right angle; the line style is a distraction.

2 Working with groups of shapes

Three of the most common similarities are...

- the number of sides or corners
- the number of items in each box
- lines of symmetry.

Identifying the similarities

Look closely at the two images to the right and see how many similarities you can find:

- All of the shapes have solid sides.
- All of the shapes are shaded white.
- Each image has a total of 12 sides and 12 corners.

Identifying the differences

Now look at the two images again and see how many differences you can find:

- The first image has three shapes, but the second has four shapes.
- The first image has three different shapes, but the second has four identical triangles.
- The second image has four lines of symmetry, but the first has none.

3 Working with segmented shapes

More complicated questions often involve segmented shapes as there are more elements to compare when looking for similarities and differences.

Look closely at the two images in the example below and see how many similarities you can find:

- Both are squares split into eight triangular segments.
- Both have black, white and spotted segments.
- All of the lines are solid.
- Both images have three black segments.

⚠ Watch out!

That looks familiar!

Compound shapes like this often have a built-in distraction because they look like an object you will recognise, such as a car or a boat.

Skills practice

Look at the shading in the two segmented images above and see how many differences you can find.

You must be able to...

- ⊙ identify all of the connections in a question
- ⊙ pick out the relevant connections
- ⊙ identify and discard the distractions.

Example

                                                    a   b   c   d   e

Look at the three images on the left. Decide what makes these three images similar to each other. Now find the image on the right that is *most like* the three images on the left. Circle the letter under the correct answer.

① Identifying all the connections

Some questions give you more information than you need. These extra pieces of information are distractions and being able to discard them is an important skill.

Look closely at the three images in the example and see how many connections you can find:

- All three boxes contain a simple arrow, but they are all pointing in different directions.
- All three boxes contain a regular shape, but they all have different types of shading.

② Picking the relevant connections

When you have connections that seem to be confusing, look at the possible answers to see whether or not they give any clues:

- All of the options have a simple arrow, but they are also pointing in different directions. This suggests it's a *distraction* – there to catch your eye and confuse you, but not relevant. Imagine the arrows are not there.
- The options all have one shape with varying shading patterns. The one shape might be relevant but the different shading patterns are not. Imagine all the shapes are shaded black.

③ Identifying and discarding distractions

Removing the distractions makes the question much easier. Have a look at the question again, ignoring the distractions and see what you can now find:

- The three images are all regular shapes.

Looking at the options, only one is a regular shape and that is image **d**.

⚠ Watch out! »»»

Common distractions

Make sure you are certain that an element is a distraction before you completely ignore it. If you think it *might* not be, just come back to it later.

Some of the most common distractions are different shading patterns and line styles in the shapes. If all of the shapes have different patterns you know it'll be a distraction. The direction an arrow is pointing in can also be a distraction.

Sometimes the shapes you see are themselves distractions, and there are other factors to consider such as the number of lines they are made out of, whether they have an odd or even number of lines, or their size or position within the box.

Skills practice »»»

Look at these five images. Work out what connects four of the images and makes the other image the odd one out. Circle the letter under the image most unlike the others.

   a   b   c   d   e

Write or underline your answers as you are instructed in each question.
Do not write answers in the 'Mark' column.

TARGET TIME
88:15
15 minutes

! Note: the questions in this test are challenging, and are intended to find out which
• skills you may need to develop to achieve success in the 11+ tests.

Look at the five images in each row. Work out what connects *four* of the images and makes the other image the odd one out. Circle the letter under the image *most unlike* the others.

Example 1

a   (b)   c   d   e

*Shapes a, c, d and e all have four sides; shape b has three sides. The shape most unlike the others is **b**.*

Mark

Now have a go at these similar questions. Circle the letter under the image *most unlike* the others.

1

    a   b   c   d   e

2

    a   b   c   d   e

3

    a   b   c   d   e

4

    a   b   c   d   e

5

    a   b   c   d   e

Example 2

Look at the two images on the left. Decide what makes these two images similar to each other. Now find the image on the right most like the two images on the left. Circle the letter under the image *most like* the others.

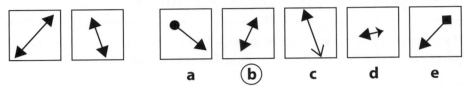

a   **(b)**   c   d   e

*The two images on the left have identical arrow heads at both ends of the line. Only **b** has the same arrow head at both ends.*

Mark

Now have a go at these similar questions. Circle the letter under the image *most like* the others.

6 a   b   c   d   e

7 a   b   c   d   e

8 a   b   c   d   e

9 a   b   c   d   e

10 a   b   c   d   e

11 a   b   c   d   e

TEST ENDS

Codes with two letters

Example 1

DV   DW   CV   BX

?   CD   DX   CW   VX   DB

a   b   c   d   e

The four images on the left each have a code. Work out how the codes go with these images. Now find the correct code from the list on the right that matches the fifth image. Circle the letter under the correct answer.

1. Identifying a common feature

Codes with two letters often represent images that have only two features that change, so the task is to link one of the letters with one of the two features. You will then know that the second letter refers to the remaining feature.

Finding the codes

Look at the letters before looking at the images. Identifying common letters will tell you which images to compare to begin working out the code:

- In Example 1, the first two shields share the same first letter, D. This tells you that they will have an identical feature.

DV   DW

- Now look at the images and try to identify the features within them:
  - DV is a shield with a curved top and a solid black line going across it diagonally.
  - DW is a shield with a straight top and a solid black line going across it diagonally.
- Once you have identified the common features you will need to check the other images and codes to see if these features match any other images:
  - In this case there are no identical lines or other codes with a D.

D represents the solid black line going across the shield diagonally.

Cracking codes by letter position

DW   CV   BX

Knowing one code often provides a shortcut to working out some remaining codes. Here we know the first letter relates to the diagonal line across the shield. In the question above...

- D is a solid line
- C is a dotted line
- B is a dashed line.

2. Working out the remaining codes

Eliminating the features

By working out the first letter of each code, it is easier to decipher the second as you have already eliminated one feature (the diagonal line in this case).

- Look for other features in the images that you haven't linked to a code. In this example, the only other changing feature is the shape of the shield. Begin with the first letter in the question – V:
  - DV is a shield with a curved top.
  - CV is a shield with a curved top as well so this must be the code for V.
- You now need to examine the shield shape linked to the remaining two code letters to work out what they represent:
  - V has a single curve at the top.
  - W has a thick black line at the top.
  - X has two curves at the top.

Cracking the code

Working out the code for each feature means that you can confidently work out the missing code for the final shield:

  ?

- Try working out the code without looking at the options and then check to make sure the option has been provided in the answers.

- The image is a shield with a dotted line going diagonally across it and a thick black line at the top. Therefore you should end up with the code CW for the fifth image.

- Answer the question as you have been instructed and circle the answer **c**.

③ Solving problems with more than two features

Example 2	HQ	IP	JR	JQ	?	HR	QI	HP	HI	JP
						a	b	c	d	e

When more than two features are present in codes with two letters the questions are slightly more difficult to answer, but the method is the same. You just have to work methodically to identify what each letter represents.

Identifying a feature with common letters

Don't be distracted by the more complex images in these questions; begin by looking at the code letters as you did before.

- First find a pair of common letters and identify the features:
  - The letter J is common to the third and fourth shapes.
  - JR is a clock with a spotted pendulum that has swung to the left. The time is about eight o'clock.
  - JQ is a clock with a spotted pendulum that is in the middle of its swing. The time is about half past two.

- When you have identified the common feature you can ignore the others and work out the rest of the code:
  - H is a black pendulum.
  - I is a white pendulum.
  - J is a spotted pendulum.

Cracking codes by letter position

You now know that the first letter is linked to the colour of the pendulum, so you can discount this feature when moving on to the second letter.

If there are more than two features, as there are in Example 2, continue to work in the same way as you did for the first part of the question, looking at each of the remaining features.

Finding the second feature

- Look for another pair of letters and identify the common features:
  - The first and fourth images in both have the letter Q in their codes.
  - HQ is a clock with a black pendulum that is in the middle of its swing. The time is about two o'clock.
  - JQ is a clock with a spotted pendulum that is in the middle of its swing. The time is about half past two.

- When you have identified the common feature you can ignore the others and work out the rest of the code:
  - All the images are clocks, so the second letter must represent the position of the pendulum, but not the shading of it.

- Check the position of the pendulum in relation to each letter:
  - P is a pendulum that has swung to the right.
  - Q is a pendulum in the middle of its swing.
  - R is a pendulum that has swung to the left.

Now you have worked out the code you can answer the question. The code for the fifth image is HP.

⚠ Watch out!

Distractions

Code questions often contain distractions to confuse you. Both the clock faces and the times in Example 2 were distractions and included to confuse you.

Skills practice

Draw the clock images out again, varying the shading on the clock faces and the position of the hands to make a new code.

Codes with three letters

Example

RJW   SKW   RKY   TJX

?   SJX   SKY   TKW   RSW   TJW

       a   **b**   **c**   **d**   **e**

The four images on the left each have a code. Work out how the codes go with these images. Now find the code from the list on the right that matches the fifth image. Circle the letter under the correct answer.

1 Identifying common letters in codes

Codes with three letters represent images with three features that change, so the task is to link the letters with one of the three features.

Work methodically to identify the codes, trying to work from left to right if you can. You can scribble notes to help you remember what each letter represents.

Finding the first code

As with two-letter codes, before looking at the images you should first focus on the letters. Common letters will tell you which images to compare. Try to find two codes that only share the first letter:

- In the example, the codes for the first and third images both begin with the letter R. This tells you that there is going to be something identical about them.
- Now look at the images and try to identify the features within them:
  - RJW has white and spotted segments on the outside with white and striped segments in the middle. The segments are in line with each other.
  - RKY has white and spotted segments on the outside with white and black segments on the inside. The segments do not line up.
- It looks like R represents the white and spotted segments around the outer circle. Now you need to check the other images and codes to see if the feature and the letter match any other images.

In this case there are no other images with white and spotted outer segments or other codes with an R, so this must be the correct answer to the code.

Cracking codes by letter position

As the first letter of the code must stand for a related feature, you can now work out the codes for the remaining first letters. In the code above, the first letter represents the shading in the outer segments:

- R is for white and spotted.
- S is for white and black.
- T is for white and striped.

2 Deciphering the second code letter

Now move on to the second letter in the code and work out which feature it represents:

- Look for other features in the images that you haven't linked to a code. There are two features that are changing – shading of the inner segments and whether or not the segments are in line with each other. As you know what the first letter represents you can ignore it for now:

SKW   RKY

  - SKW has white and striped inner segments which are not in line with the outer segments.
  - RKY has white and black inner segments which are not in line with the outer segments.

The common feature is that the segments are not in line with each other.

- You now need to examine the images to work out the letters for the middle of the code:
  - J shows the segments are in line with each other.
  - K shows the segments are not in line with each other.

3 Working out the remaining codes

RJW   SKW

Finally you are ready to tackle the third code letter, and at this stage there should be only one possible feature left:

- Look for two images that share their final code letter. In this case we have two that share the letter W. As you know the features for the first two letters you can ignore them:

  ▪ RJW has white and striped inner segments.

  ▪ SKW has white and striped inner segments.

Therefore white and striped inner segments are represented by the letter W.

- You now need to examine the images linked to the remaining two code letters to complete the code:

  ▪ W is for white and striped.

  ▪ Y is for white and black.

  ▪ X is for white and spotted.

?

Working out the code for each letter means that you can confidently work out the missing code for the final image.

Try working out the code without looking at the options and then check to make sure the option has been provided in the answers:

- The image has white and striped segments on both the inside and outside, and the segments are in line with each other.

- The code for those features is TJW.

Answer the question as you have been instructed. In this case you should circle the answer **e**.

Quick tips

When the images look like an object you recognise, such as a car or boat, it is often easier to think of each feature as a part of that object when you are comparing them. In the images below, the triangle looks like a sail, the straight line looks like a mast and the quadrilateral looks like the hull of a boat.

Things change!

Sometimes two codes can represent different aspects of the same feature. In the example on page 19, both the first and last letter refer to segment shading. They use the same shading styles for different parts of the image.

The two images above both show a square with a circle in it, the only difference is whether or not the segments line up. This change is easy to see but when shading patterns are introduced, this difference is harder to spot.

Star-shape questions often use shading for codes but also for positioning, so one of the letters might refer to a point having a particular style of shading. If this was a two-letter code, one letter might be the position of the black point and the other the position of the spotted point.

Orientation is another aspect to consider. Look at image above to work out the direction in which the small triangles are pointing. With this sort of question, look for a horizontal or vertical line to find which way the shapes point in.

Skills practice

Copy these blank images on to paper and make up codes of your own. You can use different shading styles, but not colours.

You can rotate the shapes so that the × in the middle becomes + and vary the number of segments that you shade.

You can always try them out on your family to see if they can do what you've got to do!

Write or underline your answers as you are instructed in each question.
Do not write answers in the 'Mark' column.

TARGET TIME

88:15

15 minutes

! Note: the questions in this test are challenging, and are intended to find out which skills you may need to develop to achieve success in the 11+ tests.

The four images on the left each have a code. Work out how the codes go with these images. Now find the correct code from the list on the right that matches the fifth image. Circle the letter under the correct answer.

Example

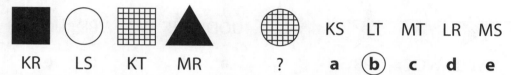

*The fifth shape is a circle and has a hatched pattern. A circle has the letter code L. A hatched pattern has the letter code T. The answer is **b**.*

Mark

Now have a go at these similar questions. Circle the letter under the code that is the correct answer.

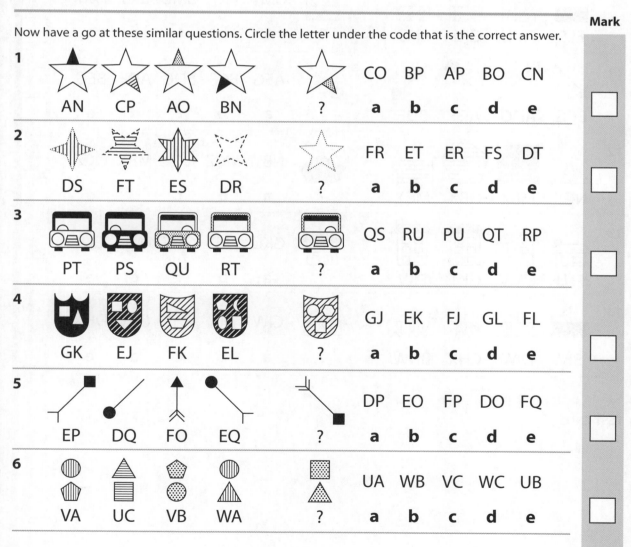

Mark

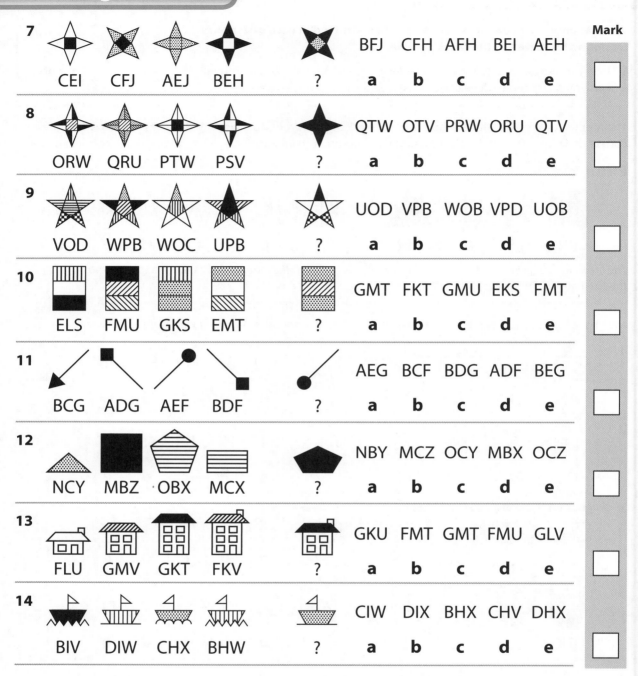

7 CEI CFJ AEJ BEH ? | BFJ CFH AFH BEI AEH
a b c d e

8 ORW QRU PTW PSV ? | QTW OTV PRW ORU QTV
a b c d e

9 VOD WPB WOC UPB ? | UOD VPB WOB VPD UOB
a b c d e

10 ELS FMU GKS EMT ? | GMT FKT GMU EKS FMT
a b c d e

11 BCG ADG AEF BDF ? | AEG BCF BDG ADF BEG
a b c d e

12 NCY MBZ OBX MCX ? | NBY MCZ OCY MBX OCZ
a b c d e

13 FLU GMV GKT FKV ? | GKU FMT GMT FMU GLV
a b c d e

14 BIV DIW CHX BHW ? | CIW DIX BHX CHV DHX
a b c d e

TEST ENDS

You must be able to...

- identify the relationship between shapes within an image
- break the relationship down into a series of connections
- apply the relationship to the shapes within another image.

Example
 → : →

a   b   c   d   e

Look at the pair of images on the left connected by an arrow. Work out how the two images go together. Now look at the third image, which is followed by another arrow. Work out which of the five images on the right completes the second pair in the same way. Circle the letter under the correct answer.

1 Identifying relationships between shapes

Changing shapes is all about spotting a range of connections. These connections together make a set of step-by-step instructions that you can apply to another image. Those connections could be…

- shading changes
- shapes moving or even swapping places
- the number of shapes
- size changes and rotations.

2 Finding the connections

Look closely at the first two images in the example. There are three changes that occur:

- The three pentagons are moved so that they are one inside the other.
- The medium-sized pentagon is then shaded black.
- The small square is then moved underneath the pentagons.

3 Applying the relationship to another image

Once you have worked out the relationship you have to apply it to a different set of shapes. Have a look at the third box. It has three circles and one triangle. You need to apply the relationship to the third box:

- Move the three circles together so that they fit one inside the other.
- Shade the medium-sized circle black.
- Move the triangle underneath the circles.

Now compare this image with the possible answers. Option **e** is a perfect match and is the correct answer.

⚠ Watch out!

One step at a time

Some of these relationships really do need the steps to be taken in the same order. This is especially true when rotations and reflections are used.

Have a look at these three boxes:

The second box is the first one rotated 90° clockwise and then reflected in a horizontal mirror line. The last box is made by taking the first box, reflecting it in a horizontal mirror line and rotating it 90° clockwise. As you can see they do not match. Find out more about reflections and rotations on pages 26–28.

Quick tips

If you find that there are too many steps to remember easily you should scribble very brief notes beside the question or draw on the question itself to help you.

Skills practice

Create a box with some shapes in that do not include circles, squares, diamonds or rectangles. Then come up with a two-step relationship that includes a reflection. See what happens as you change the order of the steps. For a bigger challenge add more steps.

You must be able to...

- identify a constant number pattern in a series of images
- identify proportions in an image
- match the proportions of one image to a different image.

Example

a   **b**   **c**   **d**   **e**

Look at the two images on the left. Decide what makes these two images similar to each other. Now find the image on the right that is most like the two images on the left. Circle the letter under the correct answer.

1. Identifying a constant number pattern

Questions that involve number patterns can be amongst the hardest to spot as you need to see more images to identify the pattern. These sorts of number patterns are covered in Simple number patterns on page 40.

The number of sides, corners or points can be as important as any other connection. The same is true of proportion, where you will commonly see segmented shapes with shading patterns. These questions will often include additional elements, such as rotation.

Look closely at the first two images in the example above and see how the shaded areas are alike:

- All of the shading is black.
- Both images have two shaded segments on the outside.
- Both images have two shaded segments on the inside.
- The shaded segments on the inside are next to each other.

2. Identifying the proportions in an image

Look at these first two images again and count how many segments there are of each type of shading. On shapes like these it's a good idea to treat the outer segments and inner segments separately:

- There are eight outer segments in each image; two are black and the remaining six are white. The ratio of black to white is 1 : 3
- There are eight inner segments in each image; two are black and the remaining six are white. The ratio of black to white is 1 : 3

3. Matching the proportions to the answer

Have a look at the possible answers and see which ones fit each connection:

- All of the options have black shading.
- Options **b**, **d** and **e** have two segments shaded on the outside.
- Options **a**, **b**, **d** and **e** have two segments shaded on the inside.
- Options **a** and **b** have the shaded inner segments next to each other.

Only option **b** fits all of the connections, so **b** is the correct answer.

This sort of question confuses a lot of people as often they don't look for enough connections. The way the inner segments are arranged is just as important as there being two inner segments that are shaded. If you think that two options **could** be the correct answer you need to look for another connection, however subtle it might be.

Quick tips

If you are struggling to find a connection, start counting the number of corners – you'll be surprised how often it's an important connection.

Skills practice

Seemingly identical objects can have differences between them. Look at two bricks on a wall that are side by side. They might be the same sort of brick but you'll see differences between them in the way they've aged and worn. How many differences can you find between them?

You must be able to...

- identify how a shape has been moved within an image
- link shapes together to form larger shapes
- apply the complete relationship to the shapes within another image.

Example

Look at the pair of images on the left connected by an arrow. Work out how the two images go together. Now look at the third image, which is followed by another arrow. Work out which of the five images on the right completes the second pair in the same way as the first pair. Circle the letter under the correct answer.

1 Identifying how a shape has been moved

When shapes travel around the box they can be moved in several different ways. The simplest movements are left to right or top to bottom. If you have two shapes they could swap places, and possibly sizes, at the same time. However, one of the most common types of change you will see is when the shapes are joined up or put on top of each other.

2 Linking shapes together

Look closely at the first two images in the example above and see if you can work out what happens to get from the first to the second image:

- The two sections are brought together.
- They are rotated 180° as one.
- The top section turns spotted.
- The bottom section turns black.
- The whole shape is moved to the bottom of the box.

When you get a question like this, watch for the peaks and troughs: they can be a clue for *rotation* or *reflection*.

3 Applying the complete relationship

Once you have the relationship worked out you need to take the third image and apply the changes to it *in the same order*:

- The two sections are brought together.
- They are rotated 180° as one.
- The top section turns spotted.
- The bottom section turns black.
- The whole shape is moved to the bottom of the box.

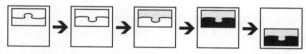

The final image matches option **a**.

⚠ Watch out! ⟫⟫⟫

Shading patterns

When shapes are brought together to make a larger shape you often have to reflect them or swap the shading patterns on them. Look at the images very carefully as these questions can be designed to catch you out.

Quick tips

While you are getting used to these questions, keep a piece of scrap paper beside you to draw the relationships as you think about them. This will help you become quicker at breaking them down.

Skills practice ⟫⟫⟫

Look at how this pair of shapes have been moved. See if you can repeat the changes on sets of shapes that you have created.

You must be able to...

- recognise a reflection in a vertical line
- recognise whether a whole image is reflected or just shapes within it
- apply the reflection to another image.

Example

                                      a   b   c   d   e

Look at the pair of images on the left connected by an arrow. Work out how the two images go together. Now look at the third image, which is followed by another arrow. Work out which of the five images on the right completes the second pair in the same way as the first pair. Circle the letter under the correct answer.

1 Recognising a reflection in a vertical line

The most common type of reflection you will see is a reflection in a vertical line.

Spotting these reflections is sometimes obvious as the shapes have all swapped sides. However, when it's just one shape in the middle of the box it's not so obvious, as with this pentagon.

When a shape is reflected through a line, every point on the shape has to 'travel' to the line as quickly as possible, and then must 'continue' past the line for exactly the same distance.

2 Recognising the reflection type

There are two types of vertical reflection: one that happens *inside* the box and one that happens *between* boxes.

Look closely at the first two images in the example at the top of the page and see if you can work out the type of reflection that is taking place:

- The star moves from the left-hand side to the right-hand side.
- The triangle moves from the right-hand side to the left-hand side.
- The shaded section of the triangle moves from the left to the right.

It looks like everything has swapped over so the whole box has been reflected in a vertical mirror line.

3 Applying the reflection to another image

Now you will need to apply the reflection to the third image.

Before looking at the possible answers, try to work out what it should look like:

- The circle moves from the left to the right.
- The arrow moves from the right to the left.
- The arrow is reflected so it has to face the other way.

The final image is a match for option **c**.

⚠ Watch out! ⟫⟫⟫

Checking reflections

When an image has several shapes or features you need to check all of them to see if you are looking at a true reflection.

Skills practice ⟫⟫⟫

Look at the first of these images closely. One of the other images is a reflection of this image, but which one is it?

                                            a   b

Reflections in horizontal and diagonal lines

You must be able to...

- identify and apply a reflection in a horizontal line
- identify a reflection in a diagonal line
- apply a reflection in a diagonal line to another image.

Example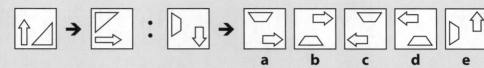

Look at the pair of images on the left connected by an arrow. Work out how the two images go together. Now look at the third image, which is followed by another arrow. Work out which of the five images on the right completes the second pair in the same way as the first pair. Circle the letter under the correct answer.

① Identifying and applying a reflection in a horizontal line

Reflections in horizontal lines are often harder to spot than those in vertical lines.

Look at the two pentagons. The second one appears to be upside down compared to the first. If you think an image might be a reflection in a horizontal line, imagine that line is just below the box. Check by making points from the image 'travel' to that reflection line by the shortest route and then continue the same distance beyond it.

One of the difficulties with reflections in a horizontal line is that the boxes are arranged side by side. However, you can sketch underneath the question.

- Take each point of each shape to the line and then the same distance beyond.
- Do this one shape at a time, and join the points up before doing the next shape.
- Match what you've sketched to the answer options.

② Identifying a reflection in a diagonal line

The most complicated type of reflection is in a diagonal line. The reason is that it appears to make the different elements rotate and move in a way that doesn't quite seem right.

Look closely at the first two images in the example at the top of the page and you'll see that the two shapes almost seem to be moving to parts of the box independently of each other.

The shapes have been reflected in a diagonal mirror line, drawn from bottom left to top right, across the box.

Remember, every point of each shape needs to reach the mirror line by the shortest possible route and continue the same distance beyond it. In the diagram you can see an arrow where five of the corners have been marked with different colours. The arrow has been reflected in the diagonal line.

③ Applying a reflection in a diagonal line to another image

Now apply the reflection to the third image in the example. Draw the shapes out and use the coloured spot trick to follow what is happening:

- The mirror line is close to the bottom of the trapezium and to the top left corner of the arrow, so these will not move as far as the rest of the shapes.
- The top of the trapezium and the right of the arrow head will move the furthest.

The final image is a match for option **d**.

⚠ Watch out!

Circles and squares

Squares and circles will always look the same once they've been reflected. If you put coloured spots on the corners of a square you will be able to see that the reflection has happened.

Skills practice ▶▶▶

Draw a box on a piece of paper and fold it so that the fold is along a diagonal. Draw shapes in one half and then try to reflect them in the mirror line.

You must be able to...

- recognise whether a rotation is clockwise or anticlockwise
- identify the size of the rotation and apply this to another shape
- work with two different rotation patterns.

Example    : →

               a   **b**   **c**   **d**   **e**

Look at the pair of images on the left connected by an arrow. Work out how the two images go together. Now look at the third image, which is followed by another arrow. Work out which of the five images on the right completes the second pair in the same way as the first pair. Circle the letter under the correct answer.

① Recognising the direction of a rotation

There are two aspects to rotations. The first is the direction of rotation, which can be clockwise or anticlockwise. If the rotation is 180° it could be either clockwise or anticlockwise (it comes to the same thing) and the direction is not important.

② Identifying and applying the rotation

The second aspect is the size of the rotation. Rotations take place in multiples of 45° or 60°, depending on the shape. With segmented shapes you will often notice that the rotation is of one or two segments, which can be easier to identify than a specific angle.

Identifying the rotation

Look closely at the first two images in the example above and see if you can work out the direction and size of the rotation that is taking place:

- The circle moves from bottom left to bottom right.
- The arrow changes from pointing right to pointing up.
- The arrow head moves from top right to top left.

It looks like the whole image has rotated 90° anticlockwise.

Applying the rotation to another image

Once you are confident you have identified the rotation you need to apply it to the third image to find the correct answer:

- If the arrow is rotated 90° anticlockwise it will go from pointing left to pointing down, with the head in the bottom right corner.

- If the parallelogram is rotated 90° anticlockwise it will go from the left to the bottom. There will be two vertical sides and two angled sides. The lowest point will be near the arrow head.

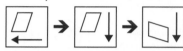

The correct answer is option **a**.

③ Working with two different rotation patterns

Some questions will use two different rotation patterns, as in this example. The shading of the outer segments rotates in one direction while the shading of the inner segments rotates in the other.

Another type of question uses a group of shapes with different shading patterns. Often the shapes will rotate around the box in one direction while the shading will go in the opposite direction.

Quick tips

Physically rotating the question, can sometimes help with spotting rotations. Arrows can give you a clue to the amount of rotation, especially if you think of them as clock hands.

Skills practice ▶▶▶

Copy these shapes on to tracing paper. Rotate the tracing paper by different amounts and try to remember how the shapes look.

Put a few coloured dots on the paper to help you see what is happening.

Write or underline your answers as you are instructed in each question.
Do not write answers in the 'Mark' column.

TARGET TIME
88:15
15 minutes

! Note: the questions in this test are challenging, and are intended to find out which skills you may need to develop to achieve success in the 11+ tests.

Look at the pair of images on the left, connected by an arrow. Work out how the two images go together. Now look at the third image, which is followed by another arrow. Work out which of the five images on the right completes the second pair in the same way as the first pair. Circle the letter under the correct answer.

Example

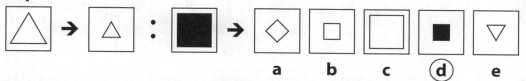

*The second shape in each pair remains the same colour and is reduced in size. The answer is **d**.*

Now have a go at these similar questions. Circle the letter under the correct answer.

Mark

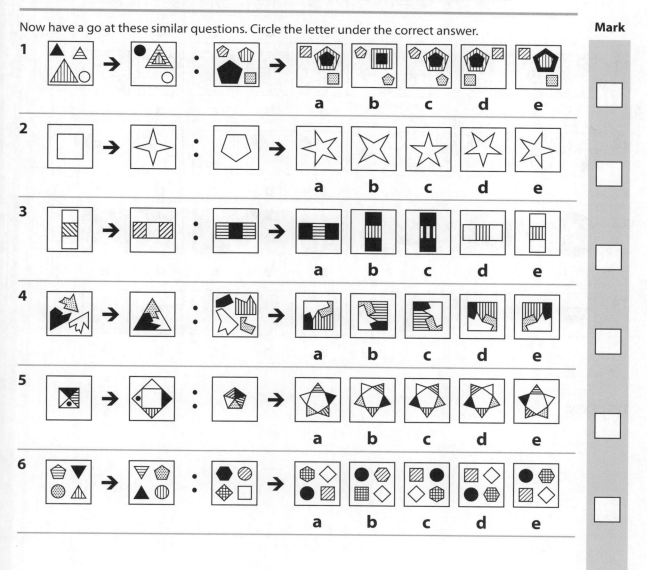

Mark

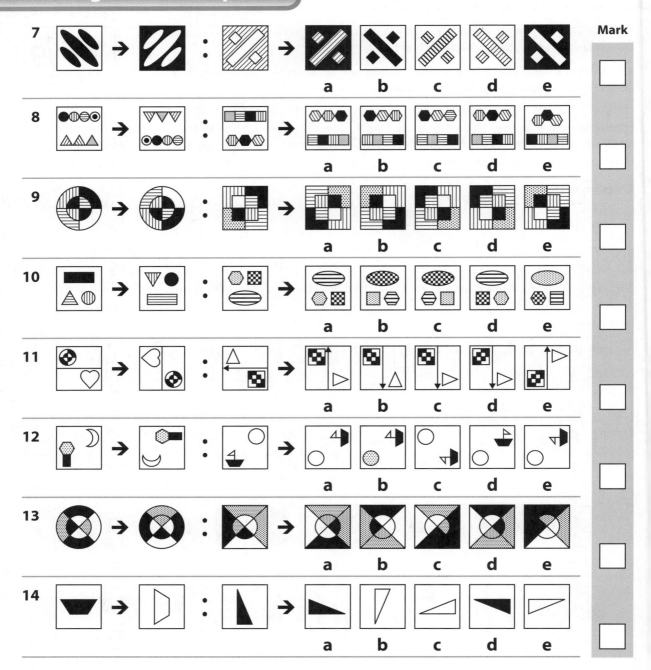

7

8

9

10

11

12

13

14

a b c d e

TEST ENDS

Simple 2 × 2 grids

You must be able to...

- identify the key box in 2 × 2 grids
- find the rules that are working within the grid
- combine the rules to find the answer.

Example

One of the boxes is missing from the grid on the left. Work out which of the five boxes on the right completes the grid. Circle the letter under the correct answer.

 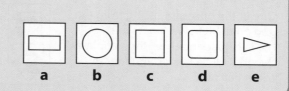

a b c d e

Identifying the key box

Simple 2 × 2 grid questions use all of the common connections and relationships, but the images that make up the question are arranged in a grid rather than in a line. In a 2 × 2 grid you will have three boxes with images and one that's blank. You need to work out which image should go into the empty box.

Have a look at the example and focus on the three boxes that have a shape inside them. Only one box is connected to the other two shapes – the box on the top left. This is the **key box**: it's the one that will help you unlock the answer.

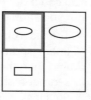

② Finding the rules within the grid

Now you need to look at how the shapes relate to the one in this key box:

- The key box has a small oval in it. The oval is wider than its height.

- The box to the right of the key box has a large oval in it. The oval is wider than its height.

The rule between these boxes is that the shape gets bigger as it goes from left to right.

Now compare the third box with the key box:

- The key box has a small oval in it. The oval is wider than its height.

- The box below the key box has a small rectangle in it. The rectangle is wider than its height.

The rule between these boxes is that the shape changes from an oval to a rectangle as it moves down the grid.

③ Combining the rules

Now that you have got the two rules you should be able to work out which of the answers is correct:

- The first rule suggests the small rectangle should become a large rectangle.

- The second rule suggests the large oval should become a large rectangle.

The two rules suggest the answer is a large rectangle. The answers is option **a**.

⚠ Watch out! ⟫⟫⟫

Don't rush!

With simple 2 × 2 grid questions you can find that the answer is sometimes fairly obvious. That's great, but take a few moments to double check it just in case there are two very similar possible answers. In the example above, options **c** and **d** look alike.

Skills practice ⟫⟫⟫

Which is the key box in this question?

Now choose your answer from the five boxes below and write an explanation for why you have chosen it.

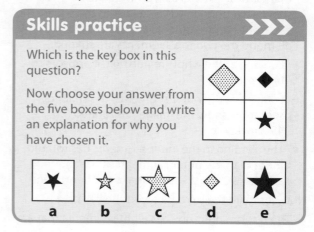

a b c d e

You must be able to...

- identify the key box in complex 2 × 2 grids
- break down the relationship to find the rules that are working within the grid
- combine the rules to find the answer.

Example

One of the boxes is missing from the grid on the left. Work out which of the five boxes on the right completes the grid. Circle the letter under the correct answer.

a   b   c   d   e

① Identifying the key box

Complex 2 × 2 grid questions combine connections and relationships to make more complex rules.

Just as with the simple grids, you need to look at the key box to unlock the question (the image connected to the other two). In the example above the key box is on the bottom left.

② Breaking down the relationship

Look at how the other two images within the grid relate to the key box. You may need to look at the rule in more than one part:

- The key box (bottom left) has eight triangular segments in it, arranged to show a square inside a diamond. In the diamond the top and right segments are shaded black. In the square the bottom and left segments are shaded black.

- The box above the key box has eight triangular segments in it, arranged to show a diamond inside a square. In the square the two right-hand segments are shaded black. In the diamond the two top segments are shaded:

  - Looking at the whole image first, it appears to have rotated.

  - Looking at the outer segments, the shaded segments show the image has rotated 45° clockwise.

  - The shading in the inner segments has rotated more than the outer segments. It has rotated another 90° clockwise to make the new image.

Now compare the third box with the key box:

- The bottom right box has eight segments that are all quarter circles. In the outer segments the right and bottom ones are shaded black. In the inner segments the top and left one are shaded black:

- Looking at the whole image, the triangles have become circle segments, but the segments of both images seem to line up with each other.

- The shaded segments have rotated 90° clockwise around the image.

③ Combining the rules

You could get the answer from using just one rule, but you should use both to check your answer:

- The first rule suggests the circular image should rotate 45° clockwise and then the shaded inner segments should rotate another 90° clockwise.

- The second rule suggests the top-left image should see the triangular segments become circular segments and then the whole image rotate 90° clockwise.

Both rules suggest concentric circles. The outer one should have both bottom segments shaded black, while the inner one should have both right-hand segments shaded black. Option **c** is correct.

Skills practice ≫≫≫

Now try this question. Work out which of the five boxes below completes the grid and write down the reason for your answer.

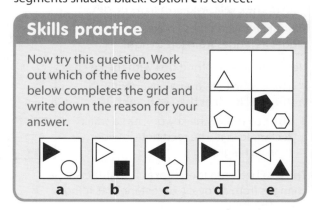

a   b   c   d   e

You must be able to...

- identify vertical and horizontal relationships within simple 3 × 3 grids
- discard the irrelevant relationships
- check that the relationships agree.

Example

One of the boxes is missing from the grid on the left. Work out which of the five boxes on the right completes the grid. Circle the letter under the correct answer.

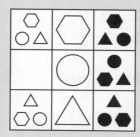

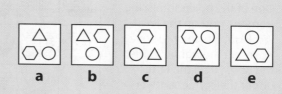

1 Identifying the relationships

You are shown nine boxes in a 3 × 3 grid and one of them is empty; you need to work out and pick the correct one from the five options provided. The simpler questions will often involve rules and relationships that work in rows and columns. Sometimes it can be as simple as the shapes increasing in size as you go down the columns. Questions can often use a change of shading pattern or a reflection.

There will be more than one relationship in the grid, even in simple questions. Have a look at the example above and see how many relationships you can spot:

- All of the shapes are hexagons, circles and equilateral triangles.
- In the third column, all of the shapes are shaded black. The others are all shaded white.
- In the third column, the position of the shapes rotates anticlockwise within the squares.
- In the first and third columns, there always appears to be one shape above the other two.
- The top shape in the first and third columns is the large shape in the middle column.
- The first column appears to be a reflection of the third column with a shading change.

2 Cutting down the options

Six different relationships is a lot for a simple question. However, with nine boxes in the grid you will often see this number of possibilities.

Look at the relationships again: the first three can all be ignored as the answer options fit the first two and the third can't apply to the first column.

Now look at the possible answers the other three leave you with:

- If there is always one shape above two others then only options **a**, **c** and **e** fit.
- If the large shape is important then you want an answer with a circle at the top. Only option **e** fits.
- If the reflection is important the circle will be at the top and the other shapes underneath. Again only option **e** fits.

3 Checking that the relationships agree

All three of the rules you have looked at give **e** as a possible option, with all of the other answers being proved incorrect by two of the rules.

It's always worth double checking. The best way to do this is to sketch beside the grid, as keeping a lot of different relationships in your head can be tricky.

Option **e** is the correct answer.

Fast-facts

Questions that use a vertical mirror line down the middle of the central column are very common.

Skills practice ▶▶▶

Look at the example again. If the bottom row moved to the middle, and all the rules stayed the same, what would the first and third rows look like?

You must be able to...

 identify vertical, horizontal and diagonal relationships within complex 3 × 3 grids

 discard the irrelevant relationships

 check that the relationships agree.

Example

One of the boxes is missing from the grid on the left. Work out which of the five boxes on the right completes the grid. Circle the letter under the correct answer.

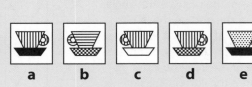

① Identifying the relationships

Complex 3 x 3 grid questions can involve relationships that work horizontally, vertically and diagonally. Some diagonal patterns can go in two different directions. For example, the shading pattern could run in the diagonal from top right to bottom left and the kind of shape from top left to bottom right. Rotational patterns are also quite common in this type of question.

Complex grid questions may have fewer relationships than the simple questions, but they will be harder to spot. It can be useful to note when you *cannot* see a relationship. Have a look at the example above and see how many similarities and differences you can find:

- All of the images look like teacups on saucers.
- Some of the teacups appear to be facing the same direction.
- There are no two teacups of the same shading pattern in any row or column.
- There are no two saucers of the same shading pattern in any row or column.
- There are no two pairs of saucers and teacups with the same shading pattern combination.
- The teacups with horizontal line shading appear to be in a diagonal line from top left to bottom right.
- The other teacups appear to follow that pattern.
- The saucer shading pattern appears to go from top right to bottom left.

② Cutting down the options

As before, quite a few of the relationships do not really give us any clue. It is only the last three rules that tell us what to look for:

- If the teacup shading pattern is moving down and to the right, look for an image of a teacup with vertical stripes. Options **a**, **c** and **d** fit this.
- If the saucer shading pattern is moving down and to the left, look for an image of a saucer with a spotted shading pattern. Options **b** and **d** fit this.

③ Checking that the relationships agree

These relationships might not seem to work together as they have focused on different parts of the image, but they do both agree on one of the possible options: **d**.

To check that option **d** is right, you should sketch beside the grid. Start by drawing a saucer and teacup as the basic shape is always the same. Then apply the shading for the teacup and follow that with the shading for the saucer. Compare your sketch with the possible answers.

Option **d** is the correct answer.

Skills practice ›››

Use a coloured pencil to draw a faint line through all of the squares where the cups have horizontal shading. Use another colour for vertical shading. Watch how the pattern jumps when you reach the edge of the

grid. Repeat this with a different colour line for each of the shading patterns and see what you get. Try to remember the pattern that you see as it will help you in the test.

Write or underline your answers as you are instructed in each question.
Do not write answers in the 'Mark' column.

TARGET TIME
10 minutes

! Note: the questions in this test are challenging, and are intended to find out which
• skills you may need to develop to achieve success in the 11+ tests.

One of the boxes is missing from the grid on the left. Work out which of the five boxes on the right completes the grid. Circle the letter under the correct answer.

Example

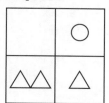   **a**   **b**   **c**   **d**   **e**

*As the shapes in the boxes move from right to left, they double in number. The correct answer is **b**.*

Now have a go at these similar questions. Circle the letter under the correct answer.

Mark

1

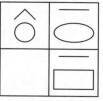   **a**   **b**   **c**   **d**   **e**

2

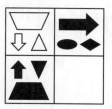   **a**   **b**   **c**   **d**   **e**

3

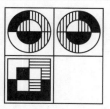   **a**   **b**   **c**   **d**   **e**

4

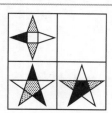   **a**   **b**   **c**   **d**   **e**

Mark

5

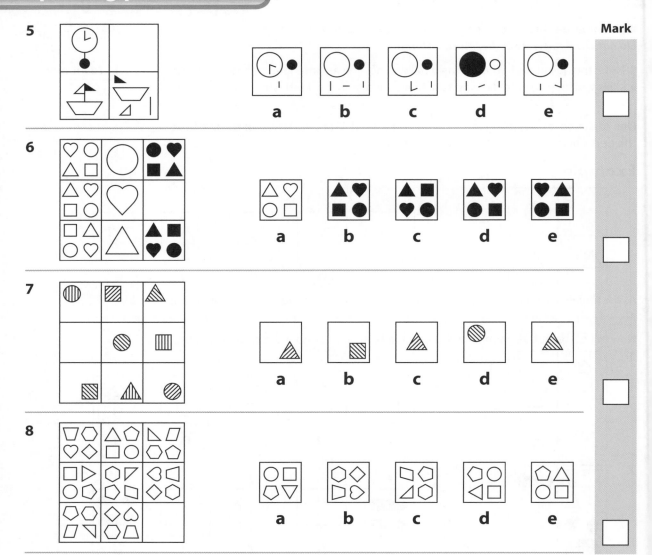

a   b   c   d   e

6

a   b   c   d   e

7

a   b   c   d   e

8

a   b   c   d   e

TEST ENDS

Repeating patterns

1 Identifying alternating patterns

Repeating patterns questions use one relationship repetitively between the five boxes on the left. These are simple patterns and often include just two images that keep swapping, like a triangle becoming a circle and then going back to a triangle.

Look at the example above:

- The first, third and fifth boxes have happy faces.
- The second box has a sad face.

To follow this pattern, the empty box should be identical to the second box.

You are looking for a sad face with no shading, which is option **c**.

2 Identifying reflecting patterns

While the example above is a simple alternating pattern, other patterns are based on reflections.

Look at these three triangles and work out what sort of reflection is happening between each pair of boxes:

- The first box has a right-angled triangle with the right angle in the bottom left of the box.
- The second box has a similar right-angled triangle with the right angle in the bottom right of the box.
- The third box matches the first box.

As you work from left to right, the shape is being reflected in a vertical mirror line.

Sometimes the repeating pattern is not as obvious as you might expect.

Look at these five boxes and work out where the reflection is in this question.

- All of the shapes are regular.
- The first and last boxes match each other.

The reflection is a vertical mirror line that goes through the middle of the third box and straight through the triangle inside it.

These sorts of patterns build up in the first three boxes before reversing in the last three boxes. The middle box is always unique.

3 Identifying extended patterns

Another common repeating pattern involves rotation. In these questions, the image will rotate a set amount from box to box, eventually returning to it's original position. The pattern will then repeat.

Look at the five boxes and work out what is happening in each box:

Because the two 'arms' of the image are of different lengths the rotation is easy to follow. The image rotates 90° clockwise between the boxes. The pattern repeats every four boxes.

Whenever you have a pattern like this with a 90° rotation, the first and last boxes will always match each other as long as there are no additional connections such as a shading pattern change.

Skills practice

Look at this sequence and describe the shape that should be in the empty box.

You must be able to...
- recognise the repeating step in a pattern
- identify all of the connections in the pattern
- apply the pattern to find the missing image.

Example

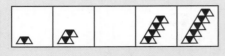

a b c d e

One of the five boxes on the right completes the sequence or pattern on the left. Circle the letter under the correct answer.

1 Recognising the pattern

One-step pattern questions have one relationship that is used repeatedly between the five boxes on the left. It could be that something – the same item or the same amount – is added each time. It could also be a combination of items, but the key here is that you are looking for the same change every time.

In the example the third box is missing, and this can be the most difficult one as three boxes in a row can make patterns easier to spot. Have a look at the other images and see if you can identify the pattern:

- The first box has three triangles in it, one black and two white.
- The second box has double the number of triangles in it, with the same proportion of black and white.
- The fourth box has four times the number of triangles as the first box, with the same proportion of black and white.
- The fifth box has five times the number of triangles as the first box, with the same proportion of black and white.

It looks like the third box should have three times the number of triangles, with the same proportion of black and white.

2 Identifying all the connections

Unfortunately, a few of the possible options fit this explanation so you need to find something else. Look again at how the triangles are arranged:

- The three triangles in the first box are in a line with the middle one upside down. Treat this as the basic block.

- The other images are made up of similar blocks on top of each other. The bottom block is always in the same place and they are arranged so that there is a straight line running up the left-hand side.

3 Applying the pattern

You are now looking for three blocks, starting in the bottom left corner with a smooth line on the left-hand side and one black triangle for every two white triangles:

- Option **a** does not have three rows.
- Option **b** fits all of the connections you've found.
- Option **c** does not have the straight line on the left-hand side.
- Option **d** has the wrong proportion of black and white shading.
- Option **e** is in the wrong place.

The correct answer is option **b**.

⚠ Watch out!

Is it just one step?

It can be very easy to spot a pattern and get carried away, so take a few moments with these questions: check the shading patterns are not swapping, or the positions are not changing.

Quick tips

One-step patterns are one of the question types where you are unlikely to see extra shapes in the box to distract you.

Skills practice

Have another look at the example. If **c** had been the correct answer, what would the fourth and fifth boxes have looked like?

Two- and three-step patterns

You must be able to...

- recognise the unique steps in a pattern
- identify all of the connections in the pattern
- apply the pattern to find the missing image.

Example

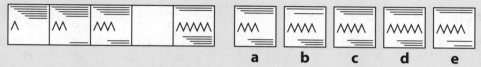

a   b   c   d   e

One of the five boxes on the right completes the sequence or pattern on the left. Circle the letter under the correct answer.

1 Recognising the unique steps in a pattern

Two-step patterns

Two-step patterns have two distinct changes taking place. Sometimes one change is a shape being built up, while the other is another shape being reduced. Usually both changes happen in each box, but sometimes one of the changes only happens in every other box, just to catch you out.

As two-step patterns have at least two different connections, it's a good idea to work on one at a time. The example above has two parts – the inverted V shapes and the lines:

- An extra inverted V is added to each box. These start on the left and are all connected to make a zigzag pattern.
- The first box has six lines at the top and none at the bottom.
- The second box has five lines at the top and one at the bottom.
- The third box has four lines at the top and two at the bottom:
  - It looks like one of the lines is moving from the top to the bottom in each box. You can use the fifth box to check this. It should have two lines at the top and four at the bottom.
  - It does, so you have found the rule.

Three-step patterns

Three-step patterns are an extension of two-step patterns but with *three* distinct changes taking place. You need to approach them in exactly the same way as two-step patterns, but find three different connections. Question 32 of the *Placement test* is an example of a three-step pattern.

2 Identifying all the connections

It's very easy to find some connections and believe you've found all of them, but always double-check. The best way to do this is to mark the question with a different symbol for each connection – a dot, a short vertical line, a short horizontal line or another similar simple mark.

3 Applying the pattern

Now you need to work out what should be in the empty box:

- There should be four inverted V shapes in the middle.
- There should be three lines at the top and three lines at the bottom.

The correct answer is option **c**.

These questions are all about the little details. Look at the way the inverted V shapes start on the left and grow across the boxes, but are always linked together.

Also have a look at the lines. While one line always moves to the bottom, the lowest one from the top moves to become the highest line at the bottom. Only one line moves at a time.

Skills practice >>>

Use some building bricks to create your own two-step patterns. Try to limit yourself to no more than two different colours per pattern. Ask your parents to create some to test you as well.

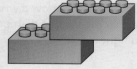

You must be able to...
- recognise a number pattern
- identify the increase or decrease from one box to the next
- apply the same changes to find the missing image.

Example

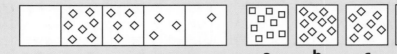

a b c d e

One of the five boxes on the right completes the sequence or pattern on the left. Circle the letter under the correct answer.

① Recognising number patterns

Simple number patterns are all about the number of shapes, sides or corners in each image and the way they increase or decrease. This will generally be a change of one or two per box, but the change is the same in every box. You have probably seen sequences like 1, 3, 5, 7, 9 and that is exactly the sort of pattern you will see in this sort of question. Patterns are based on addition, subtraction and multiplication, although multiplication is rarer.

Look at the images above and see if you can work out the pattern:

- The first box is empty.
- The second box has seven diamonds in it.
- The third box has five diamonds in it.
- The fourth box has three diamonds in it.
- The fifth box has one diamond in it.

The number of diamonds is decreasing by two as you move from left to right.

② Identifying the increase or decrease

One of the great things about simple number patterns is that you usually know what you are looking for quickly.

In this example, going from left to right, it looks like two diamonds are removed each time.

③ Applying the changes

Two diamonds are removed when you go from left to right, so that means two diamonds are added as you go from right to left.

As the second box has seven diamonds in it you need to find an answer with an extra two diamonds:

- Option **a** has nine squares in it.
- Option **b** has ten diamonds in it.
- Option **c** has eight diamonds in it.
- Option **d** has ten squares in it.
- Option **e** has nine diamonds in it.

The diamonds in the example are just squares that have been rotated 45°, but in all of the boxes in the question the diamonds are all identical so the correct answer is option **e**.

⚠ Watch out! ⟫⟫⟫

Use all of the information

It's a common trick to put the right number of the wrong shape as one of the possible answers, just to see if you're focusing on the whole question and not just the number sequence.

Skills practice ⟫⟫⟫

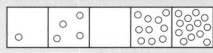

Which of the boxes below completes the sequence or pattern above?

Write a short explanation for why you have chosen your answer.

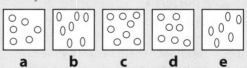

a b c d e

Square and triangular number patterns

You must be able to...

- recognise square and triangular number sequences
- solve problems with square number sequences
- solve problems with triangular number sequences.

Example 1

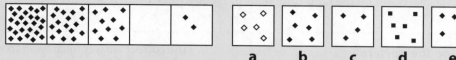

One of the five boxes on the right completes the sequence or pattern on the left. Circle the letter under the correct answer.

1 Recognising square and triangular number sequences

A *square number* is what you get when you multiply a number by itself:

- $2 \times 2 = 4$ means that 4 is a square number.
- The first ten square numbers are 1, 4, 9, 16, 25, 36, 49, 64, 81 and 100.

Questions that use square number patterns will often have lots of small shapes, with each box having a square number of shapes. The sequence could be increasing or decreasing.

The sequence of *triangular numbers* is based on adding up all of the whole numbers from 1 to whichever triangular number you want.
For example…

- to get the third triangular number you have to do the sum $1 + 2 + 3 = 6$.
- the first ten triangular numbers are 1, 3, 6, 10, 15, 21, 28, 36, 45 and 55.

Questions that use triangular numbers work in the same way as those with square numbers.

2 Solving problems with square number sequences

Identifying the pattern

Look at the five boxes in Example 1 and make a note of the contents of each one:

- The first box has twenty-six black diamonds in it.
- The second box has seventeen black diamonds.
- The third box has ten black diamonds in it.
- The fourth box is empty.
- The fifth box has two black diamonds in it.

Ignore the last box for now and focus on the first three:

- To get from twenty-six to seventeen you take away nine.
- To get from seventeen to ten you take away seven.
- The difference appears to be decreasing by two each time.

Checking your ideas

If the *difference* between boxes is decreasing by two each time, then five shapes must be removed from the third box to get the fourth box. In turn, three shapes must be removed from the fourth box.
You need to ask if that will leave two shapes in the last box:

- Box three has ten black diamonds in it. Removing five would leave five black diamonds in the empty box.
- If you now take away three from the remaining five you will be left with two black diamonds in the last box, which matches what you can see.

The correct answer must have five black diamonds in the box. Option **e** is the only possible answer.

 Watch out!

Extra connections

Sometimes there could be another connection on top of the square number pattern, such as the shapes changing from one box to another or a rotation.

Quick tips

If you have discounted an answer, put a little faint cross at the top to help yourself remember.

Fast facts

If the number of shapes in each box increases by two more than the previous increase, you have a square number sequence.

③ Solving problems with triangular number sequences

Example 2

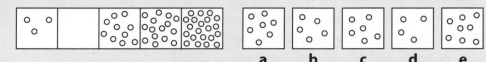

One of the five boxes on the right completes the sequence or pattern on the left. Circle the letter under the correct answer.

Identifying the pattern

Have a look at the five boxes above and make a note of the contents of each one:

- The first box has three circles.
- The second box is empty.
- The third box has ten circles.
- The fourth box has fifteen circles.
- The fifth box has twenty-one circles.

Ignore the first box for now and focus on the last three:

- To get from ten to fifteen you have to add five.
- To get from fifteen to twenty-one you have to add six.
- The difference appears to be increasing by one each time.

Checking your ideas

If the *difference* is increasing by one each time, then the difference between the second and third boxes must be four, and from the second to the first box must be three. You need to ask if that gives the correct number of circles in the first box:

- Box three has ten circles in it. If you take away four you would have six circles in the second box.
- If you take away three from the six you are left with three circles in the first box, which is correct.

The correct answer must have six circles in the box. Option **c** is the only possible answer.

You might have noticed that the sequence in the boxes is part of the triangular number sequence 1, 3, 6, 10, 15… and so worked out straight away that the number of circles in the second box must be six.

This wouldn't have been so easy to see if this sequence had been, for example 4, 6, 9, 13, 18 (with one number missing).

 Watch out!

Information overload

Keep an eye out for triangular pattern questions that use different shading patterns as the number of each pattern might be important. The shapes are so small that they are likely to just be black and white shapes.

Quick tips

The boxes in the questions can only hold a limited number of shapes, so you are unlikely to have to remember more than the sequence of triangular numbers to twenty-eight.

Fast facts

If the number of shapes in each box increases by one more than the previous increase, you have a triangular number sequence.

Skills practice

Which of the boxes on the right completes the sequence or pattern on the left? Write a short explanation for why you have chosen your answer.

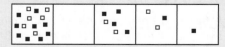

Completing sequences *test*

Write or underline your answers as you are instructed in each question.
Do not write answers in the 'Mark' column.

TARGET TIME
88:15
15 minutes

! Note: the questions in this test are challenging, and are intended to find out which
● skills you may need to develop to achieve success in the 11+ tests.

One of the five boxes on the right completes the sequence or pattern on the left. Circle the letter under the correct answer.

Example

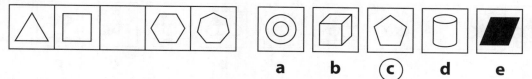

a   b   ⓒ   d   e

Looking at the boxes from left to right, the number of sides on the shape increases by one each time. The correct answer is **c**.

Mark

Now have a go at these similar questions. Circle the letter under the correct answer.

1

a   b   c   d   e

2

a   b   c   d   e

3

a   b   c   d   e

4

a   b   c   d   e

5

a   b   c   d   e

6

a   b   c   d   e

Mark

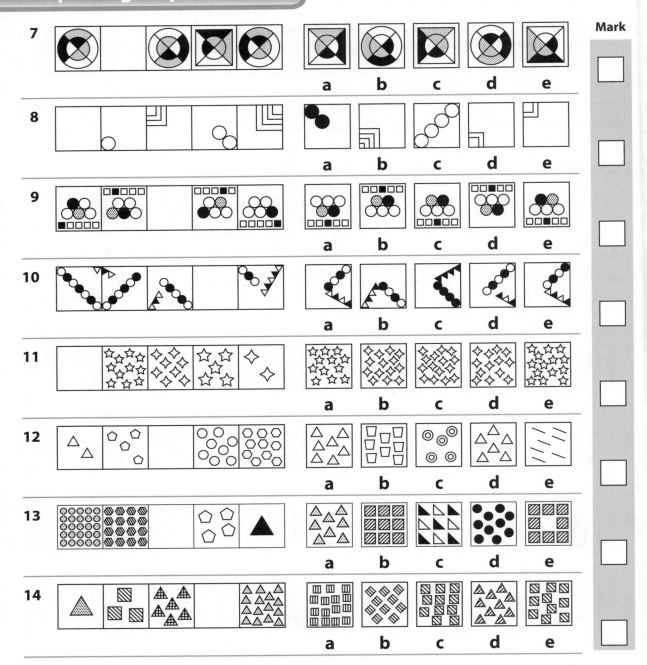

Placement *test*

Write or underline your answers as you are instructed in each question.
Do not write answers in the 'Mark' column.

TARGET TIME
88:45
45 minutes

! Note: the questions in this test are challenging, and are intended to find out which skills you may need to develop to achieve success in the 11+ tests.

Making connections

Look at the five images in each row. Work out what connects *four* of the images and makes the other image the odd one out. Circle the letter under the image *most unlike* the others.

Example

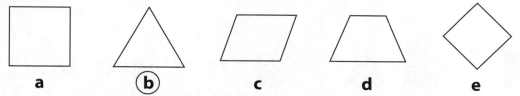

*Shapes a, c, d and e all have four sides; shape b has three sides. The shape most unlike the others is **b**.*

Mark

Now have a go at these similar questions. Circle the letter under the image that is *most unlike* the others.

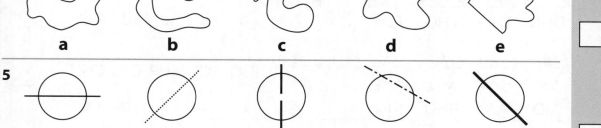

6

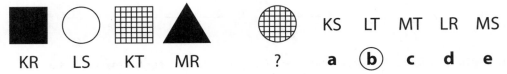

| a | b | c | d | e |

Mark ☐

Breaking codes

The four images on the left each have a code. Work out how the codes go with these images. Now find the correct code from the list on the right that matches the fifth image. Circle the letter under the correct answer.

Example

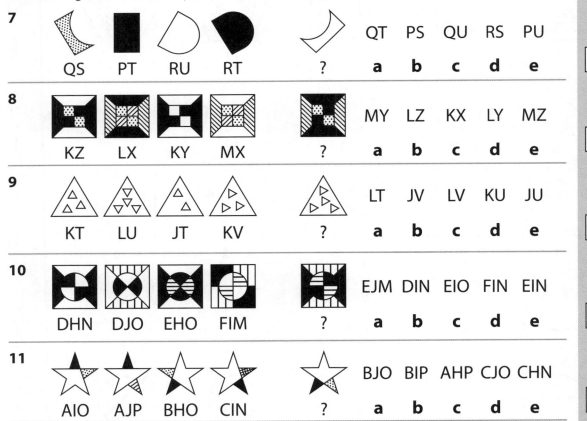

The fifth shape is a circle and has a hatched pattern. A circle has the letter code L. A hatched pattern has the letter code T. The answer is **b**.

Now have a go at these similar questions. Circle the letter under the correct answer.

© Letts Educational, *an imprint of HarperCollins Publishers*

Finding relationships

Look at the pair of images on the left, connected by an arrow. Work out how the two images go together. Now look at the third image, which is followed by another arrow. Work out which of the five images on the right completes the second pair in the same way as the first pair. Circle the letter under the correct answer.

Example

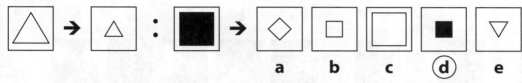

*The second shape in each pair remains the same colour and is reduced in size. The answer is **d**.*

Now have a go at these similar questions. Circle the letter under is the correct answer.

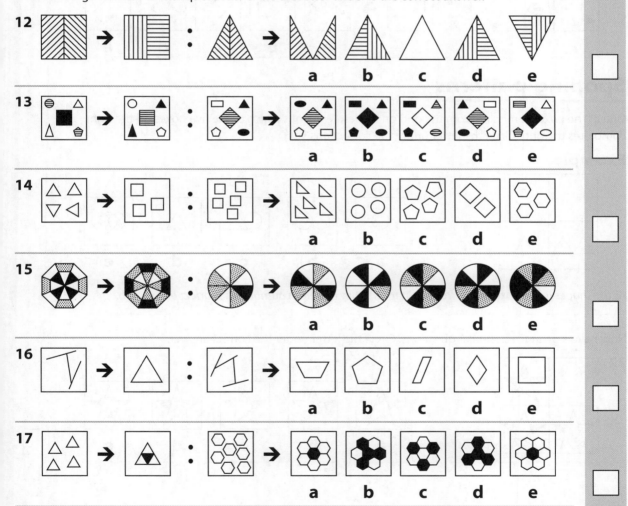

Mark

Mark

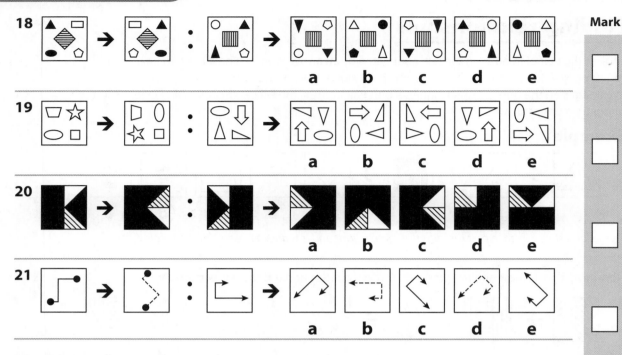

Spotting patterns

One of the boxes is missing from the grid on the left. Work out which of the five boxes on the right completes the grid. Circle the letter under the correct answer.

Example

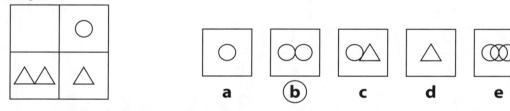

*As the shapes in the boxes move from right to left, they double in number. The correct answer is **b**.*

Now have a go at these similar questions. Circle the letter under the correct answer.

22

Mark

23

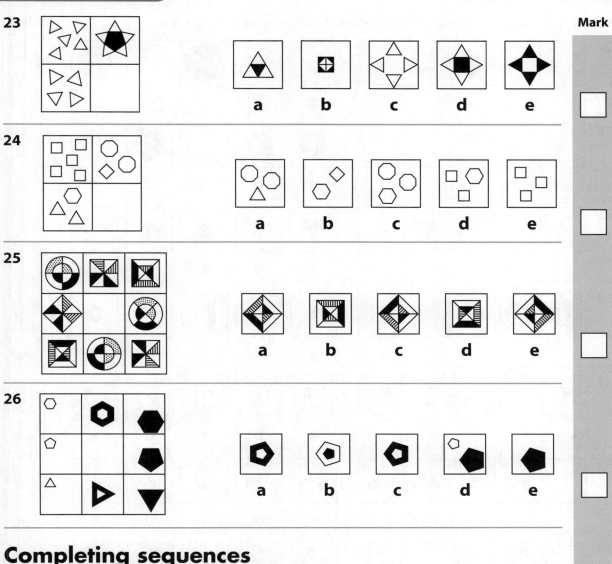

24

25

26

Completing sequences

One of the five boxes on the right completes the sequence or pattern on the left. Circle the letter under the correct answer.

Example

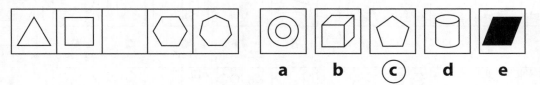

*Looking at the boxes from left to right, the number of sides on the shape increases by one each time. The correct answer is **c**.*

Now have a go at these similar questions. Circle the letter under the correct answer.

Mark

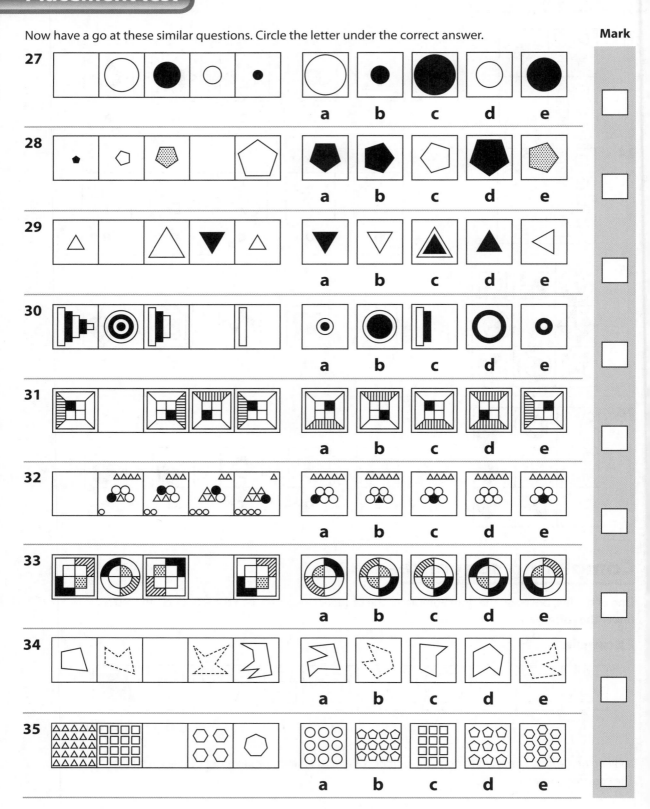

27   a   b   c   d   e

28   a   b   c   d   e

29   a   b   c   d   e

30   a   b   c   d   e

31   a   b   c   d   e

32   a   b   c   d   e

33   a   b   c   d   e

34   a   b   c   d   e

35   a   b   c   d   e

TEST ENDS

Placement test *answer grid*

Follow the instructions on pages 4–5 to fill in and use this grid.

Test results		Practice planner				
Question	Error	Skill	Page	To do	Achieved	Time (mins)
		Question types and strategies	6			60

Making connections

Question	Error	Skill	Page	To do	Achieved	Time (mins)
1		Common connections	10	17 mins	7 mins	
2						
3		Connections of direction, angle and symmetry	11	30 mins	15 mins	
4		Finding similarities and differences	13	17 mins	7 mins	
5		Spotting distractions	14	17 mins	7 mins	
6						
		Making connections test	15			15

Breaking codes

Question	Error	Skill	Page	To do	Achieved	Time (mins)
7		Codes with two letters	17	35 mins	15 mins	
8						
9						
10		Codes with three letters	19	35 mins	20 mins	
11						
		Breaking codes test	21			15

Finding relationships

Question	Error	Skill	Page	To do	Achieved	Time (mins)
12		Changing shapes	23	25 mins	15 mins	
13						
14		Number and proportion	24	20 mins	10 mins	
15						
16		Moving and connecting shapes	25	20 mins	10 mins	
17						
18		Reflections in vertical lines	26	17 mins	7 mins	
19		Reflections in horizontal and diagonal lines	27	25 mins	15 mins	
20		Rotations	28	25 mins	15 mins	
21						
		Finding relationships test	29			15

Spotting patterns

Question	Error	Skill	Page	To do	Achieved	Time (mins)
22		2 × 2 grids *Review both simple and complex.*	31	35 mins	14 mins	
23						
24						
25		3 × 3 grids *Review both simple and complex.*	33	38 mins	18 mins	
26						
		Spotting patterns test	35			10

Completing sequences

Question	Error	Skill	Page	To do	Achieved	Time (mins)
27		Repeating patterns	37	17 mins	7 mins	
28						
29						
30		One-step patterns	38	20 mins	10 mins	
31		Two- and three-step patterns	39	25 mins	15 mins	
32						
33						
34		Simple number patterns	40	17 mins	7 mins	
35		Square and triangular number patterns	41	28 mins	13 mins	
		Completing sequences test	43			15

Total [ ] Count up the boxes that you **have not** put crosses in and write this total in the box.

Total practice time [ ]

$$\frac{\text{Total test score}}{35} \times 100 = \boxed{} \%$$

Follow the instructions on page 5 to fill in and use these grids.

Making connections *test*

Question	Error	Skill	Page	Notes	Review ✗	Achieved ✓
Example 1						
1		Common connections	10			
2		Connections of direction, angle and symmetry	11			
3						
4		Finding similarities and differences	13			
5		Spotting distractions	14			
Example 2						
6		Common connections	10			
7		Connections of direction, angle and symmetry	11			
8						
9		Finding similarities and differences	13			
10						
11		Spotting distractions	14			

Total [ ] Count up the boxes that you **have not** put crosses in and write this total in the box.

$\dfrac{\text{Test score}}{11} \times 100 =$ [ ] %

Breaking codes *test*

Question	Error	Skill	Page	Notes	Review ✗	Achieved ✓
1						
2						
3		Codes with two letters	17			
4						
5						
6						
7						
8						
9						
10		Codes with three letters	19			
11						
12						
13						
14						

Total [ ] Count up the boxes that you **have not** put crosses in and write this total in the box.

$\dfrac{\text{Test score}}{14} \times 100 =$ [ ] %

Practice tests *answer grids*

Follow the instructions on page 5 to fill in and use these grids.

Finding relationships *test*

Page 29

Question	Error	Skill	Page	Notes	Review ✗	Achieved ✓
1		Changing shapes	23			
2		Number and proportion	24			
3						
4		Moving and connecting shapes	25			
5						
6		Reflections in vertical lines	26			
7						
8		Reflections in horizontal and diagonal lines	27			
9						
10						
11						
12						
13		Rotations	28			
14						

Total ⬜ Count up the boxes that you **have not** put crosses in and write this total in the box.

$\dfrac{\text{Test score}}{14} \times 100 = $ ⬜ %

Spotting patterns *test*

Page 35

Question	Error	Skill	Page	Notes	Review ✗	Achieved ✓
1		Simple 2 × 2 grids	31			
2						
3						
4		More complex 2 × 2 grids	32			
5						
6		Simple 3 × 3 grids	33			
7		More complex 3 × 3 grids	34			
8						

Total ⬜ Count up the boxes that you **have not** put crosses in and write this total in the box.

$\dfrac{\text{Test score}}{8} \times 100 = $ ⬜ %

Completing sequences *test*

Page 43

Question	Error	Skill	Page	Notes	Review ✗	Achieved ✓
1		Repeating patterns	37			
2						
3		One-step patterns	38			
4						
5		Two- and three-step patterns	39			
6						
7						
8						
9						
10						
11		Simple number patterns	40			
12						
13		Square and triangular number patterns	41			
14						

Total ⬜ Count up the boxes that you **have not** put crosses in and write this total in the box.

$\dfrac{\text{Test score}}{14} \times 100 = $ ⬜ %

Placement test

Making connections

1 **b**: the images are made up of three similar shapes, the medium shape having a striped shading pattern. The stripes in shape **b** go in the opposite direction.

2 **c**: all the shapes have six sides except for **c**, which has five sides.

3 **a**: all of the angles are acute other than **a**, which is obtuse.

4 **e**: the only shape with a straight line in it is shape **e**.

5 **d**: the only circle without a line through the middle is circle **d**. The style of the line is a distraction.

6 **d**: all of the shapes have an even number of sides except for **d**, which is a triangle and has three sides (an odd number).

Breaking codes

7 **c**: Q, P and R are the codes for the shape – a curve that looks like it takes a bite out of the rectangle, a rectangle, a curve that turns the rectangle into a 'D' shape. S, T and U are the codes for the shading – spotted, black or white. The fifth shape is a curve that goes into the rectangle (Q) and is white (U). The answer is QU.

8 **b**: K, L and M are the codes for the shading of the outer segments – black and white, black and striped, white and striped. Z, X, and Y are the codes for the shading of the inner segments – black and spotted, spotted and striped, black and white. The fifth image is shaded black and striped in the outer segments (L), black and spotted in the inner segments (Z). The answers is LZ.

9 **c**: K, L and J are the codes for the number of small triangles – three, four or two. T, U and V are the codes for the direction the small triangles are pointing – up, down or right. The fifth shape has four small triangles (L) pointing to the right (V). The answer is LV.

10 **e**: D, E and F are the codes for the shading of the inner segments – black and white, black and striped or white and striped. H, J and I are the codes for the shading of the outer segments – black and white, white and striped or black and striped. N, O and M are the codes for the crosses – whether they do not overlap, overlap and are diagonal or overlap and are vertical. The fifth shape has black and striped inner segments (E), black and striped outer segments (I), and the crosses do not overlap (N). The answer is EIN.

11 **a**: A, B and C are the codes for which point is shaded black – top, bottom left or bottom right. I, J and H are the codes for which other segment is shaded – I is top right, J is bottom right, H is top left. O, P and N are the codes for the shading of the non-black point – spotted, striped or chequered. The fifth shape's black point is in the bottom left (B), the other shaded segment is in the bottom right (J) and it has spotted shading (O). The correct answer is BJO.

Finding relationships

12 **b**: sections of the image that had a diagonal pattern that went down and to the right are given a pattern with horizontal lines. Sections of the image that had a diagonal pattern that went up and to the right are given a pattern with vertical lines.

13 **c**: the shapes within the box stay in the same position but the shading changes. The shapes that were black become striped, those that were striped become white, and those that were white become black.

14 **c**: the first box has four three-sided shapes; this changes into three four-sided shapes. The five four-sided shapes become four five-sided shapes.

15 **e**: the segments of the image that were white become spotted, those that were spotted become black, and those that were black become white.

16 **e**: the three identical lines within the box build an equilateral triangle so the four identical lines build a square.

17 **a**: the shapes in the first box are joined together and the shape in the middle is shaded black. The outside shapes are not rotated.

18 **d**: the whole box is reflected in a vertical mirror line.

19 **e**: the box is reflected in a diagonal mirror line going from top left to bottom right.

20 **c**: the white triangle rotates 90° clockwise. The shaded triangle rotates 90° anticlockwise.

21 **d**: the image is rotated 135° clockwise; the line goes from being solid to being dashed.

Spotting patterns

22 **c**: as the image in the box moves from left to right, the two small shapes swap places and then the whole image, including the small shapes, is reflected in a vertical mirror line.

23 **d**: the triangles in the left-hand box are brought together in the right-hand box and the space in between them is shaded black.

24 **e**: the shapes in the left-hand box have the same number of corners (or sides) as the shapes in the right-hand box. The top row have 20, the bottom row have 12.

25 **c**: as the images move down a row they rotate 45° clockwise and move one box to the left.

26 **a**: the first column has small white shapes in the top left corner of the boxes. The last column has large black shapes in the bottom right corner of the boxes. The middle column contains an image in the centre of the box made up of the white shape in the middle of the black shape. The images rotate 90° clockwise from one column to the next.

Completing sequences

27 **c**: the circle gets smaller from left to right. The colour alternates from box to box.

28 **b**: the pentagons get bigger from left to right. The shading pattern changes from black to white to spotted, then black (in the missing box) and back to white. The pentagons also rotate 90° anticlockwise in each box.

29 **a**: the pattern is symmetrical about the middle box. The image in the second box will be identical to the one in the fourth box.

30 **b**: the boxes all show a series of discs, some from the side and some from face on. The smallest disc is removed as you go across the boxes.

31 **a**: the shading in the outer segments of each image rotates one segment anticlockwise, while the shading in the inner segments rotates one segment clockwise.

32 **e**: as you move one box to the right, the black circle is replaced with a triangle. The next circle in a clockwise direction is turned black. A white circle is added in the bottom left and a triangle is removed from the top right.

33 **c**: the images alternate between squares and circles, but all are in eight segments. The shading of the outer segments rotates one segment clockwise, and the angle of the striped shading rotates anticlockwise about the middle of the shapes as it moves. The shaded inner segment rotates one segment anticlockwise each time.

34 **d**: the number of sides in each shape increases by one in each box from left to right. The shapes also alternate between solid and dashed lines.

35 **d**: the number of shapes in each box is the (decreasing) sequence of square numbers from 25 to 1. The shapes in each box gain one side from one box to the next.

Skills practice

Question types and strategies

Question type 6 and recording your answers 9

13 arrows. The thirteenth arrow will match the first arrow.

Making connections

Common connections 10

d: options **a**, **b**, **c** and **e** have eight sides; option **d** has seven sides. All the shapes have acute, obtuse and reflex angles and there is no obvious difference between them.

Connections of direction, angle and symmetry 12

c: options **a** and **b** have a vertical reflection and option **c** has a horizontal reflection.

Finding similarities and differences 13

The shading is different in the two images. The white segments in the first image are black in the second. The spotted segments in the first image are white in the second. The black segments in the first image are spotted in the second. In this example the link is the sequence used for the shading changes. You would expect this kind of pattern in repeating sequences.

Spotting distractions 14

d: this is the only triangle containing a right angle. The line styles are distractions.

Breaking codes

Codes with two letters 18

There are many possible answers to this question.

Codes with three letters 20

There are many possible answers to this question.

Finding relationships

Changing shapes 23

There are many possible answers to this question.

Skills practice *answers*

Number and proportion — 24
There are many possible answers to this question.

Moving and connecting shapes — 25
There are many possible answers to this question.

Reflections in vertical lines — 26
Box **b** is a reflection.

Reflections in horizontal and diagonal lines — 27
There are many possible answers to this question.

Rotations — 28
There are many possible answers to this question.

Spotting patterns

Simple 2 × 2 grids — 31
c: the key box is the black diamond shape in the box on the top right of the grid. The answer is **c** because the shape enlarges and changes from black to spotted as it moves right to left.

More complex 2 × 2 grids — 32
d: the shape in the left-hand box is rotated 90° clockwise, the shading is changed to black and the shape moves up. A shape with one more side is then added to the bottom right corner of the box.

Simple 3 × 3 grids — 33

The middle row moves to the top and the top row moves to the bottom.

More complex 3 × 3 grids — 34

Completing sequences

Repeating patterns — 37
The shape rotates 90° anticlockwise from one box to the next. The shading pattern changes from white to black to spotted and back to white.

 The missing shape should be shaded black and should look like this:

One-step patterns — 38

Two- and three-step patterns — 39
There are many possible answers to this question.

Simple number patterns — 40
d: each box has three more circles in it than the previous box. The missing box should have seven circles in it.

Square and triangular number patterns — 42
a: the sequence is the pattern of triangular numbers going down from 15 to 1. Looking at the pattern from right to left, the first square is black. In the next box the new squares are white. The middle box has new squares added in black. The missing box has more white squares added so should have six white and four black squares.

Practice tests

Making connections *test* 15
1   **e**: all of the shapes have 9 sides except for **e**, which has 11.

2   **a**: all of the arrows point upwards except for **a**, which points downwards.

3   **d**: all of the shapes have at least one line of symmetry except for **d**, which has no lines of symmetry.

4   **b**: the circles all have one inner segment and one outer segment that is unshaded except for **b**.

5   **a**: all of the shapes have straight line shading patterns except for shape **a**, which has a chequered pattern. It is also the only shape that contains right angles.

6   **c**: the group of shapes in each of the first three boxes have 11 straight sides in total. Box **c** is the only one to match this.

7   **d**: the first two shapes are isosceles triangles. Box **d** is the only one with an isosceles triangle in it.

8   **a**: all of the individual shapes in the first two boxes have vertical lines of symmetry. Box **a** is the only other box where both shapes also have a vertical line of symmetry.

9   **b**: the images are made up of a square surrounded by isosceles triangles. The triangles are split into two segments which are separated by their shading pattern. As you go clockwise around the image the first segment of each triangle is shaded to match the square. The second segment of each triangle has a different shading pattern to the first segment. All of the second segments match each other.

10 **d**: the car headlights on the first three images are all white. Car **d** is the only answer that matches this. All of the other shading and the position of the steering wheel are distractions.

11 **e**: the first two boxes contain shapes with lines that are a regular dashed pattern. Shape e is the only shape with the same pattern.

Breaking codes *test* 21
1   **a**: A, C and B are the codes for which point of the star is shaded – top, bottom left or bottom right. N, P and O are the codes for the shading – solid black, spotted or striped. The bottom-right point on the fifth star is shaded (C) and the shading pattern is spotted (O). The answer is CO.

2   **a**: the first letter is for the type of star: D – four-pointed; F – five-pointed; E – six-pointed. The second letter is for the shading pattern: S – vertical stripes; T – horizontal stripes; R – white. The orientation of the stars and patterns around their edges are distractions. The fifth shape is a five-pointed star (F) and white (R).The answer is FR.

3   **d**: the images all look like the front of a car.

The first letter is for the side the steering wheel is on: P – the steering wheel is on the left; Q – the steering wheel is on the right; R – the steering wheel is not visible. The second letter is for the body shading (but not the roof): T – white; S – black; U – spotted. The shading of the windscreen banner and the roof are distractions. The steering wheel on the fifth shape is on the right (Q) and has a white body (T). The answer is QT.

4   **c**: the first letter describes the shape of the top of the shield: G – double curve; E – straight; F – single curve. The second letter describes the number of shapes on the shield: K – two shapes; J – three shapes; L – four shapes. The shading on the shields is a distraction. The fifth shape has a single curve on the shield (F) and has three shapes inside it (J). The answer is FJ.

5   **c**: the first letter describes the tail of the arrow: E – one fin; D – no fins; F – two fins. The second letter describes the head of the arrow: P – diamond head; Q – round head; O – triangular head. The orientation of the arrows is a distraction. The fifth shape has two fins (F) and a diamond head (P). The answer is FP.

6   **e**: the first letter is for the combination of shapes: V – circle and pentagon; U – square and triangle; W – circle and triangle. The second letter is for the shading: A – vertical stripes; C – horizontal stripes; B – spotted. The shading and position of the shapes are distractions. The fifth image has a square and triangle (U) and is spotted (B). The answer is UB.

7   **c**: the first letter is for the shading of the centre of the image: C – black; A – spotted; B – white. The second letter is for the orientation: E – vertical/horizontal; F – diagonal. The third letter is for the shading of the triangles: I – white; J – spotted; H – black. The fifth shape has a spotted centre (A), has a diagonal orientation (F) and the triangles are shaded black (H). The answer is AFH.

8   **b**: the first letter is for the shading of the second half of each triangle as you go in a clockwise direction around the image: O – black; Q – striped; P – white. The second letter is for the shading at the centre of the image: R – striped; T – black; S – white. The third letter is for the shading of the first half of each triangle as you go in a clockwise direction around the image: W – white; U – spotted; V – black. The fifth image has the second half of each triangle shaded black (O), the centre of the image is black (T) and the first half of the triangle is black (V). The answer is OTV.

9   **a**: the first letter is the shading on the top triangle of the star: V – striped; W – spotted U – black. The second letter is for a vertical line of symmetry: O – there is a vertical line of symmetry; P – there is no vertical line of symmetry. The third letter is for the shading on the lowest two triangles: D – chequered; B – striped; C – white. The shading of the pentagon in the middle and the higher two triangles are distractions. The fifth shape has a black triangle at the top (U), a vertical line of symmetry (O) and the lower triangles are chequered (D). The answer is UOD.

10 **b**: the first letter is for the middle block of each image: E – no shading; F – striped; G – spotted. The second letter is for the bottom block: L – black; M – striped; K – spotted.

The third letter is for the top block: S – striped; U – black; T – spotted. The fifth shape has a striped middle block (F), a spotted bottom block (K) and a spotted top block (T). The answer is FKT.

11 **e**: the first letter describes whether the arrow is pointing up or down: B – down; A – up. The second letter is for the style of the arrow head: C – triangular head; D – diamond head; E – round head. The third letter describes whether the arrow is pointing left or right: G – left; F – right; . The fifth shape is pointing down (B), has a round arrow head (E) and is pointing to the left (G). The answer is BEG.

12 **e**: the first letter is for the basic shape: N – triangle; M – quadrilateral; O – pentagon. The second letter is for whether or not the shape is regular: C – irregular; B – regular. The third letter is for the shading of the shape: Y – spotted; Z – black; X – striped. The fifth shape is a pentagon (O), is irregular (C) and is shaded black (Z). The answer is OCZ.

13 **b**: the images all look like houses. The first letter is for whether or not the house has a chimney: F – it has a chimney; G – it does not have a chimney. The second letter is for the number of floors: L – one floor; M – two floors; K – three floors. The third letter is for the shading of the roof: U – white; V – striped; T – black. The fifth shape has a chimney (F), two floors (M) and a black roof (T). The answer is FMT.

14 **e**: the images all look like a boat at sea. The first letter is for the wave style: B – the waves are pointed; D – there are no waves; C – the waves are curved. The second letter is for the sail: I – the sail is pointing to the right; H – the sail is pointing to the left. The third letter is for the colour of the hull of the boat: V – black; W – striped; X – spotted. The fifth shape has no waves (D), a sail pointing to the left (H) and a spotted hull (X). The answer is DHX.

Finding relationships *test* 29

1 **a**: the shape in the top left-hand corner changes to match the size and shape of the bottom-right corner shape, although it retains its original shading pattern. The larger of the two other shapes moves under the smaller one and they swap shading patterns.

2 **c**: the square changes into a star with the same number of points. The points of the star are along a line from the centre of the original square through the middle of each side. As the square has a horizontal edge at the top, the star must point straight up.

3 **b**: the image rotates 90° clockwise. The shading pattern on the middle segment swaps with the other segments. The angle of the pattern is rotated with the image. The thickness of the lines does not change.

4 **d**: the segments rotate and join together to form a larger shape. The segments stay in the same area of the box.

5 **b**: the segments fold out and the shading moves one segment clockwise.

6 **e**: the shapes are reflected in a vertical mirror line and, after the reflection, the shading styles move to the next shape anticlockwise.

7 **d**: the image is reflected in a vertical mirror line and the shading style of the shapes within it swaps with that of the background.

8 **b**: the shapes are reflected in a horizontal mirror line running through the middle of the box. The shading in the group of four shapes moves one shape to the right, while the shading in the group of three shapes moves one shape to the left. The shading patterns are not reflected.

9 **e**: the image is reflected in a horizontal mirror line.

10 **c**: the whole box is reflected in a horizontal mirror line. Once reflected, the shading pattern moves to the next shape in an anticlockwise direction.

11 **c**: the box is reflected in a diagonal mirror line going from bottom left to top right. The segmented shape is a distraction as it doesn't look like it has been reflected at all, merely translated.

12 **a**: the box is reflected in a diagonal mirror line going from top left to bottom right.

13 **d**: the shading patterns on the outer segments of the image rotate 90° clockwise while the shading patterns on the inner segments rotate 90° anticlockwise.

14 **c**: the shape rotates 90° anticlockwise and the shading changes from black to white.

Spotting patterns *test* 35

1 **d**: the line in the second column becomes a corner before it moves to the first column. The other shape is turned into a regular shape, keeping the same height as the original. There is still a gap between the shapes.

2 **b**: to get from the top row to the bottom row, the shapes are reflected in a horizontal mirror line and the shading changes. If it was white it becomes black, and if it was black it becomes white.

3 **c**: the images in the first column are reflected in a vertical mirror line into the second column.

4 **a**: all the segments of the star that were white in the first column are spotted in the second column. The segments that were spotted become black and the ones that were black become white.

5 **c**: the image in the first column is taken apart in the second column. For the 'clock' image this means that the circle for the face, the hand section, the pendulum arm and the pendulum itself are all separated. Nothing is rotated.

6 **e**: the grid has a vertical mirror line running down the middle of the second column. The first column is reflected in that line to become the third column before being shaded black.

7 **c**: from one row to the next the shapes move one box to the right, but the shading patterns move one box to the left. All of the first row shapes are in the top left of their boxes, the second row shapes are in the middle of their boxes and the bottom row shapes are in the bottom right of their boxes.

8 **a**: the shapes in each box work as one image. Each image moves down to the next row, moves one box to the left and rotates 90° clockwise.

Completing sequences *test* 43

1 **c**: the shapes in the box alternate between a striped circle and a chequered oval. The missing shape is a chequered oval.

2 **d**: the shapes are symmetrical in a vertical mirror line that goes through the third box, so the shapes in the second and fourth boxes are identical and the shapes in the first and last box should be identical. The missing shape is a spotted square.

3 **d**: the shapes all look like regular shapes that have been squashed horizontally. Going from left to right, the shapes lose one side in each box. The missing shape is a tall pentagon. The shading is a distraction.

4 **b**: the shading pattern inside the diamond rotates 45° anticlockwise in each box. The missing shape is a diamond with vertically striped shading. The arrows are a distraction.

5 **a**: moving left to right, two squares are removed from each box and an octagon is added at the top. The squares are removed from the top, working from left to right on each row.

6 **c**: the triangle is reflected in a horizontal mirror line in each box. Whenever it points upwards it has a grid shading pattern; when it points down it has a chequered pattern. The pentagon is reflected in a horizontal mirror line in every second box, with the direction of shading reflecting as well.

7 **e**: the shading pattern of the inner segments rotates one segment clockwise while the shading of the outer segments rotates one segment anticlockwise. The outer shape switches between being a circle and a square.

8 **d**: the boxes alternate between a growing square pattern and a repeating circle pattern. The circles rotate around the box in an anticlockwise direction, while the squares go in a clockwise direction.

9 **c**: moving left to right, the squares move from the bottom to the top of each box and back again. The black square moves one along to the right. The circles do not move but the spotted shading moves one circle clockwise while the black one moves two circles anticlockwise. When the same circle should have both types of shading only the black is seen.

10 **a**: moving left to right, one circle becomes a triangle. The triangle closest to the edge of the box changes its shading between white and black each time and the other triangles alternate along the line. The whole shape rotates 90° anticlockwise from one box to the next.

11 **b**: moving left to right, the number of shapes in each box decreases by three each time. The shapes alternate between four- and five-pointed stars.

12 **d**: the number of shapes in each box is two more than the last. The specific shapes are distractions.

13 **b**: the boxes have the sequence of square numbers in them with twenty-five shapes in the first box, sixteen in the second and so on. There should be nine shapes in the empty box. The shading of all the shapes inside any box should be the same. The specific shapes are distractions.

14 **e**: the boxes alternate between having triangles and squares in them. The number of shapes is the sequence of triangular numbers so the fourth box should have ten squares in it. Neither squares nor triangles rotate, which excludes option **b**. The shading patterns are a distraction.